Historical Association Studies

Britain in the 1930s

Historical Association Studies

General Editors: Muriel Chamberlain and H. T. Dickinson

The Historical Association, founded in 1906, brings together people who share an interest in, and love for, the past. It aims to further the study and teaching of history at all levels: teacher and student, amateur and professional. This is one of over 100 publications available at preferential rates to members. Membership also includes journals at generous discounts and gives access to courses, conferences, tours and regional and local activities. Full details are available from The Secretary, The Historical Association, 59a Kennington Park Road, London SE11 4JH, telephone: 0171–735 3901.

Britain in the 1930s
The Deceptive Decade

Andrew Thorpe

BLACKWELL
Oxford UK & Cambridge USA

First published 1992
Reprinted 1995

Blackwell Publishers Ltd
108 Cowley Road
Oxford OX4 1JF, UK

Blackwell Publishers Inc.
238 Main Street
Cambridge, Massachusetts 02142
USA

British Library Cataloguing in Publication Data

A CIP catalogue record for this book is available from the British Library.

Library of Congress Cataloging-in-Publication Data

Thorpe, Andrew
    Britain in the 1930s: the deceptive decade/Andrew Thorpe.
        p.   cm. – (Historical Association studies)
    Includes bibliographical references and index.
    ISBN 0–631–17411–7 (pbk.)
    1. Great Britain – History – George V, 1910–1936.   2. Great Britain –
History – George VI, 1936–1952.   3. Great Britain – History – Edward
VIII, 1936.   I. Title.   II. Series.
    DA578.T45 1992
    941.08 – dc20   91–26102
                                                                                                CIP

Typeset in 11 on 13 pt Erhardt
by Setrite Typesetters Ltd, Hong Kong
Printed and bound in Great Britain by
Hartnolls Limited, Bodmin, Cornwall
This book is printed on acid-free paper

Contents

Acknowledgements

Thanks are due to Dr Joseph Smith, who first suggested that I write this book, and Dr John Critchley, my Head of Department at Exeter, for his constant help, encouragement, and tolerance. Professor Muriel Chamberlain, General Editor of the Series, and the staff of Blackwell Publishers were patient and helpful throughout. My parents, once again, were good enough to let me escape to the north from Exeter so that I could work in peace, and Jody, now my wife, ensured that I was never bored, if occasionally distracted. Finally, I would like to pay tribute to the two men who first interested me in the history of Britain in the 1930s: the late Denys R. Nicholls, my teacher at Henry Fanshawe School, Dronfield; and the late Richard Shackleton, my Special Subject tutor at the University of Birmingham, whose death at an early age has robbed many students of an incomparable teacher. They would, I am sure, have disagreed passionately with much of the content, but would, I hope, have enjoyed it just the same. It is to their memory that the book is dedicated.

1

Introduction

Britain in the 1930s was controversial at the time and has remained controversial ever since. On that, at least, there would be little disagreement. But go beyond the platitudes and there are all manner of debatable issues. In economic terms, there are questions ranging from how far government was responsible for, or could have mitigated the effects of, mass unemployment, to how far 'new' industries were replacing 'old'. There are disputes about the performance of Britain's governments between 1929 and 1940 and, in particular, as to why the National Governments dominated politics after 1931. In recent years social history has become one of the fiercest arenas of debate, with issues such as health and housing exciting hard fought and occasionally bitter exchanges.

In some ways this book follows naturally from my doctoral research on the British general election of 1931. Despite the passage of time, and the opening of archives, there had never been a systematic, archive-based study of that most fascinating of political interludes. It occurred to me then that there had been instead a gradual accretion of myth and counter-myth, whose purpose was less to enlighten than to justify the positions adopted by different people at the time. The claim of the *Manchester Guardian*, that the country had experienced during the 1931 election 'the shortest, strangest, and most fraudulent campaign of our times', was seen by many as a truism, rather than as the embittered reaction of a newspaper editor whose old Liberal certainties had been overturned by the rational decision of the electorate. As the National Government's reputation withered in the 1940s and 1950s, the election which confirmed them in power came to be seen as a fraud and a sham.

The 1930s suffered a not dissimilar fate. The political disagreements of the time were severe, and this has always been reflected in the historiography. For one thing, the decade was followed by a period of full employment, advances in social welfare both during the Second World War and the tenure of the first majority Labour government (1945–51), and, from the early 1950s, by great prosperity. This coincided, in turn, with the government's use of Keynesian demand management techniques. This seemed to suggest that Keynesianism meant full employment and that other strategies meant unemployment. John Maynard Keynes had been around in the thirties, and so had politicians advocating 'Keynesian' policies, like David Lloyd George and Sir Oswald Mosley. At the same time, the 'idealism' of the 1940s was contrasted with the 'materialism' and 'selfishness' of the preceding decade. Therefore, it followed, inter-war governments had been criminally negligent: if only they had listened to the 'lost leaders' there would not have been the omnipresent million jobless between 1920 and 1940. The same was true in foreign affairs: Churchill had predicted war and urged preparation; the National Government had not listened; the Second World War had been the consequence. Once again the incompetence of inter-war government was revealed.

This view persisted in the two decades following 1945, helped by the fact that the men who had dominated government in the later 1930s – Chamberlain, Simon, Hoare, and Halifax – were all effectively removed from domestic politics by the end of 1941. There were few ready to defend the record of the 1930s: and the fact that the Conservative party was led between 1940 and 1963 by three men – Churchill, Eden, and Macmillan – who had been rebels for at least part of the thirties meant that little attempt at rehabilitation could be expected from that quarter.

2

This all gave a clear run to critics, and a rather pessimistic view of the thirties as the 'Devil's Decade' held the field. Wartime criticisms that 'We have failed because of our selfishness, and we need a new standard of morality' (Acland, 1940, p. 31) were apparently confirmed by the Labour landslide of 1945. Mowat, ten years later, recognized that there had been some rise in living standards, but his view was effectively summed up in the comment that Britain between 1922 and 1940 had been under 'the rule of the pygmies', men like Baldwin who had marginalized greater men like Lloyd George (1955, p. 142). Ten years further on, Taylor took a not dissimilar line in his volume in the Oxford History of England series (1965); and two years after that, Skidelsky took the process to an extreme, when, in a study of the second Labour government, he attacked fiercely its failure to implement a Keynesian policy (1967).

By the late 1960s, however, three processes were at work which helped to reverse the trend. For one thing, the opening of government archives for the 1930s, following the introduction of the thirty-year rule in 1967, tended to show the governments of the thirties in a more favourable light, since they revealed the extent of their ingenuity and innovation in policy-making and also gave a clearer picture of the complexities involved. Private archives were also being opened: massive biographies of Baldwin and MacDonald in particular helped to improve their public image (Middlemas and Barnes, 1969; Marquand, 1977). At the same time there were new and less flattering portraits of some of the supposed inter-war 'giants'. It became possible, for example, to criticize Churchill (Rhodes James, 1970). Thirdly, Keynesian methods were becoming less effective: the economy stagnated and unemployment and inflation both crept upwards. It came to be realized that such methods were not a panacea, and that, in fact, post-war prosperity had been due largely to post-war phenomena – the need for reconstruction, the temporary eclipse of competitors like Germany and Japan, the influx of American aid, and favourable terms of trade. None of these factors was present in the thirties, or from the later sixties. Meanwhile, growing criticism of the

3

welfare state, not just from the reviving radical right but also from sections of the left which pointed out its failure to 'cure' poverty, suggested that thirties' government might have been justified in trying to restrict social services expenditure.

This led to changing perspectives on the 1930s. Stevenson argued in 1976 that the old ritualistic condemnations of the thirties must be at least qualified, and that there must be recognition 'of the significance of a decade which saw for many the beginning of affluence, the evolution of the welfare state, and a confirmation of the stability of British politics' (1976, p. 108). The following year he and Cook presented a wide-ranging reappraisal of the decade which again took a basically 'optimistic' view (1977). Meanwhile, the work of social historians like Winter was tending to confirm their findings (1979).

But the pessimists were not finished; and the election of the Conservative government in 1979 gave them a new lease of life. The new government's rhetoric was strikingly similar to that of the National Governments: market forces, individual responsibility, the restriction of welfare expenditure. Inflation and financial instability were now seen as bigger enemies than unemployment. The result was a renewed concern by some on the left to discredit the governments of the 1930s, for fear that, otherwise, the Conservatives' policies would seem reasonable. This was a clear motivation, for example, behind Gray's medley of random reminiscences of the thirties: 'only by remembering the past [can we] interpret the present and plan for the future' (1985, pp. 4–9). Similarly, Webster (1982) and the journal *History Workshop* were keen to present the thirties in an unfavourable light in order to delegitimize Thatcherism. Condemning the thirties became a left-wing virility symbol: anyone who took a different view was seen as a 'right-winger', as I found in discussing the work of Stevenson (who could hardly be characterized as a Thatcherite) with a colleague of Webster's in 1988. This shows how bitterly historians are divided on the subject even now.

In this book I give a brief account of the economy, politics and society of Britain in the 1930s. The conclusions are basically 'optimistic', though by no means uncritical. I would not wish to be characterized as a 'right-winger' for the line I take. History does not teach us 'lessons'; it does not prescribe action. This book is about the 1930s. It is certainly not a veiled manifesto for what its author wants to see happening in the 1990s. It should be read in that spirit.

2

Politics

British politics between 1929 and 1940 were often turbulent.
The period began with the election of the second minority
Labour government, in the last inter-war election to see a
realistic three-party contest. However, like governments in every
other major democracy, it was unable to overcome the slump
which began in 1929, and by 1931 it was on the verge of
ignominious defeat. By that time the Conservatives had recovered, but their victory came about in a most unexpected
way. In August the Labour government, unable to agree on
measures to meet a financial crisis, split; it was replaced by
a National Government under the former Labour premier,
Ramsay MacDonald, and backed mainly by Conservatives and
Liberals. That October it won an overwhelming victory at
the polls. That victory was repeated four years later, and the
National Government remained in office until the fall of Neville
Chamberlain, in May 1940, brought forth a new and more
wide-ranging Coalition under Winston Churchill.

The politics of this period have aroused much controversy.
In this chapter the five major groupings are discussed with a
view to explaining the National Government's hegemony and
the lacklustre nature of the opposition that faced it.

The 1930s were dominated politically by the National Governments, which were themselves dominated by Conservatives. That party in turn was led by two men who would provide ample ammunition for the critics of the 'Devil's Decade': Baldwin and Chamberlain. Stanley Baldwin (1867–1947), leader between 1923 and 1937, and Prime Minister 1923–4, 1924–9, and 1935–7, as well as effective deputy premier 1931–5, seemed to many to personify the age. A Worcestershire foundry owner, he had made little impact on national politics until 1922, when he took a leading role in the Conservatives' withdrawal from the Lloyd George Coalition. The following year, he became party leader. His basic approach was consensual: he generally respected his Labour opponents and had some appreciation of working-class sensibilities. Above all, he was keen to preserve democracy and capitalism, and to ensure that the Conservative Party played the leading role in that process: hence he aimed to squeeze out the disruptive third force of the Liberals and to ensure Labour's moderation. He did this by trying to play down distinctively 'Conservative' policies unless they were attractive *across* party lines. Although he cultivated a rather homely, bumbling image, he was also a very shrewd operator – parallels could be drawn with two later American presidents, Eisenhower and Reagan. In many ways, especially in his mastery of the media, Baldwin was a 'modern', adaptable, and able politician; but in retrospect his moderation and unwillingness to act hastily could be characterized as sloth and incompetence, although his image has improved in recent years (Middlemas and Barnes, 1969; Ball, 1988).

Neville Chamberlain (1869–1940), who was Chancellor of the Exchequer 1931–7 and Prime Minister 1937–40, had little of Baldwin's tact and, indeed, little patience with Baldwin himself. He possessed many of the characteristics of his distinguished father, Joseph, but was arguably a shrewder politician. Another latecomer to national politics, he quickly established a fearsome reputation as an administrative reformer. But, being

7

raised in a city (Birmingham) where his policies rarely faced serious opposition, he lacked Baldwin's conciliatory manner. His quickness to gloat over the difficulties of his opponents, and his inflexibility, made him very unpopular with them; while his cocksureness regarding the merits of capitalism and the rightness of his policies meant that his reputation sank very low once these seemed to have failed. Together, Baldwin's apparent bumbling and Chamberlain's hostility towards anything which was idealistic, or not narrowly practical, were to damage the reputation of 1930s governments for many years after their demise.

However, the Conservatives began the decade in crisis. In May 1929, after nearly five years in office, Baldwin called a general election. Most Tories expected victory, although with a majority reduced from the 200 achieved in 1924. Rejecting what he saw as the dangerous flashiness of the Liberal and Labour programmes, Baldwin fought instead on a policy of 'safety first', arguing that the country should be given a period of calm in which to allow the natural forces of economic recovery to do their work. However, despite gaining more votes than Labour, the party gained fewer seats. Baldwin refused to bargain with the Liberals he had hoped to destroy, and resigned at once.

This was Baldwin's second defeat in three general elections, and there was soon a strong movement to oust him, helped by the fact that the defeat of moderate MPs in marginal seats had swung the balance in the parliamentary party to the right. Baldwin's reluctance to move quickly towards a fully protectionist programme aroused great ire, and the press barons, Lords Beaverbrook and Rothermere, added fuel to the fire by forming an Empire Crusade Party which opposed official Conservatives in a number of by-elections in 1930 and early 1931. However, Baldwin's position should not be misunderstood. He had been a protectionist since the 1890s, but, always nervous of 'democracy', was afraid that protectionism would lose votes and saddle the country with many years of non-Conservative government, which he believed would be disastrous. In fact, the sheer intensity of the economic slump meant a rapid movement of business and public opinion towards tariffs, so that in October 1930 the party adopted a programme of protection with imperial preference. This led, incidentally, to the withdrawal from the Shadow Cabinet of the lifelong free-trader, Winston Churchill, although he waited until the more credible issue of India arose in January 1931 to announce his resignation: from then onwards he was excluded from the party's leading circles and only a party or national disaster could make him leader, as, in fact, was to happen in 1940. Though the press barons continued their campaign against Baldwin in increasingly personal terms, the focus of criticism shifting from his weakness over trade policy to his support for the Labour government's liberal policy over India, the main crisis had passed.

This was confirmed in February and March 1931 with the adoption by Baldwin of a more critical policy on India, the increasing intensity of the national crisis which helped reunite the party around demands for severe curbs on government expenditure, and evidence that the party's continuing divisions were strengthening the position of Labour at by-elections. Helped by the lack of an obvious successor, the inherently strong position of a Conservative leader, and the victory of his candidate over an Empire Crusader at the Westminster St George's by-election in March, Baldwin cemented his position as leader. By the early summer of 1931 the party was on target for a victory on the scale of that of 1924 with a four-tier policy of public economy, protection, imperial preference and assistance to agriculture, and it seemed that the prospect of a Liberal defection, led by Sir John Simon, would enable the Conservatives to oust Labour in the near future (Ball, 1988). The only real worry was a rumour that the Prime Minister, Ramsay MacDonald, favoured a 'National' government; however, Conservative leaders were adamantly against the idea and in any case it seemed to be more a sign of desperation on MacDonald's part than a viable option.

That summer, however, saw an acute financial crisis which led to demands for large cuts in public expenditure in order to balance the budget and so keep the pound on the gold standard. Because the minority Labour government would need opposition support to pass any programme of cuts, the Conservatives and Liberals were drawn into extensive negotiations. With Baldwin on holiday, Chamberlain represented the Conservatives. Although hostile to the idea of a National Government, it became clear to him that it would be advantageous if some Labour ministers could be persuaded to remain in office to pass the cuts, so spreading their unpopularity and reducing working-class hostility towards his own party. When the National Government was formed by MacDonald on 24 August, there were four Conservatives, including Baldwin and Chamberlain, in the ten-man Cabinet.

Allegations that the Conservatives had plotted the formation of a National Government were absurd. While accepting that they had a patriotic duty to serve, most Conservatives harboured deep doubts and suspicions, and wanted the government to be a purely temporary expedient to balance the budget before an election was called on party lines at which they would be able to advance their protectionist programme. However, the next six weeks saw a rapid movement of opinion, so that on 5 October the National Cabinet supported a National appeal by the existing government against Labour. A number of reasons accounted for this apparently breathtaking shift. The Labour party's swing to the left, once in opposition, worried Conservative leaders, who began to see the possibility of a Labour government as the prelude to a national catastrophe, while the splits and disorganization within that party made an early election seem attractive (all the more so if National co-operation could maximize straight fights against Labour). Secondly, MacDonald and some other non-Conservatives in the government were ready to accept tariffs and other aspects of the Conservative programme. Thirdly, the forced departure from the gold standard in September seemed to increase the need for an early resolution of political uncertainty. Fourthly, Baldwin found working as second-in-command to MacDonald very congenial, and saw co-operation with non-Conservatives as a way of weakening his party's right wing. Finally, the Conservative Party and press were becoming increasingly hysterical in their demands for an early election, and there was nothing so obnoxious about the government as to make its demise preferable to an early election against Labour. The Conservatives had hoped to fight on a protectionist programme: to this end they hoped to replace the free-trade Liberals with the more tariff-inclined Liberal Nationals under Sir John Simon. However, the refusal of MacDonald to be a party to the free-traders' expulsion, and their own refusal to be expelled, meant that the government called instead for a 'doctor's mandate' or 'free hand' to use any methods it saw fit to restore the adverse balance of trade and end the slump.

Ramsay MacDonald (1866–1937) was a curious figure to find at the head of such a government. A low-born, illegitimate Scot, he had struggled for years before becoming the first Secretary of the Labour Party. During the First World War he had been ostracized for what was seen as an 'anti-war' stance; between 1922 and 1931 he had been leader of the party and, as one contemporary observer put it, 'like Lenin, . . . the focus for the mute hopes of a whole class' (Wertheimer, 1929, pp. 176–7). Yet he had never been a class warrior. In the 1900s he had been keen to co-operate with the Liberals; his conception of socialism had always been vague. More to the point, he had long held two beliefs: that socialism would evolve from the success of capitalism, and that Labour and he should prove themselves 'fit to govern'. His actions in 1931, therefore, were less of a departure than his astonished erstwhile admirers alleged. Capitalism was in crisis: 'sound' economic policies were needed to restore it to health and resume the advance towards socialism. He would show, also, that he was 'fit to govern' by trying to solve the problems faced rather than by resigning. But MacDonald was already past his prime, and he would soon find himself an isolated, declining, and despised figure dependent on Baldwin's loyal support for his hold on the premiership.

The election campaign of 1931 was marked by vitriol and scare stories on both sides, but these were of secondary importance. Labour's image suffered from the record of the 1929–31 government, its leaders' conduct in failing to support

11

MacDonald, and its unconvincing policies. By contrast, the National Government had a broad appeal; and the Conservatives' protectionism (most National candidates were Conservatives), which they advocated widely despite the 'doctor's mandate', gave it a convincing and well-worked-out policy for insulating Britain from the worst effects of the world slump, perhaps even for restoring a prosperity little known since the First World War. This was emphasized by the fact that unemployment fell during the campaign itself, because of increased business confidence (due to the formation of the National Government) and the devaluation of the pound (which had made British exports cheaper). In the event the government won a landslide victory; 470 of its 554 MPs were Conservatives (see Appendix 1). There would be National Governments, increasingly dominated by the Conservatives, until the dark days of 1940 brought forward a more wide-ranging coalition still.

Although the National Government went on to win a less comprehensive, but hardly less convincing, victory in November 1935, it would be wrong to understate the administration's difficulties in the interim. The nature of the National Government itself was one of the main problems. After the 1931 election, the Cabinet was restored to full size. Of its twenty members, eleven were Conservatives, four National Labour, three official (Samuelite) Liberals and two Liberal Nationals (Simonites). This in no way reflected the parliamentary balance, and there were periodic Conservative stirrings against such a distribution of the top jobs, not least because it meant that many Tories who could have expected Cabinet office in a party administration did not achieve it. Too much could be made of this, of course. MacDonald remained premier, but worked hand-in-glove with Baldwin. The Samuelite Liberals, known free-traders, were confined to non-economic posts. In fact, all the key economic jobs went to Conservatives, with the exception of the Board of Trade; and that went to a Liberal National, Walter Runciman, who was seen as reasonably co-operative. Chamberlain, the arch-protectionist, became Chancellor of the Exchequer.

The heterogeneity of the Cabinet was especially problematical during the government's first year in office. The Samuelites had dashed Tory hopes when they had not resigned before the election. They did not object strongly when an emergency tariff was imposed in November 1931, but they threatened to resign over the proposed introduction of a permanent system of protection the following January. This would have been an embarrassing split so soon after the election. To prevent it, the Cabinet made an 'agreement to differ', an unprecedented suspension of the convention of collective responsibility on the single issue of trade policy. Parliament was thus treated to the somewhat bizarre spectacle of Liberal ministers opposing their own government from the front bench in the debates on the Import Duties Bill; the bill was passed, but it was clear that a breach could not be long delayed. Finally, when a system of imperial preference was agreed with the Dominions at Ottawa in September 1932, the free-traders resigned, with relief all round. When one of them had died in July, he had been replaced by a Conservative; now a Conservative and a Liberal National were brought in to fill the vacant places. When the Cabinet reverted to twenty in December 1933, a Conservative benefited; and when Baldwin, having succeeded MacDonald in June 1935, formed an even larger Cabinet, it comprised fifteen Conservatives, four Simonites and three National Labourites. This represented a subtle yet perceptible shift. The National image was maintained, but there was little to distinguish the National Labourites or the Liberal Nationals by 1935. They added variety and flavour, but not much else: for example, the ailing MacDonald had become an embarrassment long before he exchanged offices with Baldwin in 1935, while Sir John Simon's performance as Foreign Secretary was lamentable. But their presence did allow Baldwin to pursue a more moderate line, on issues like India, than might have been the case under a single-party administration. By the time of the 1935 election, though, MacDonald and Simon had been reshuffled to less importance posts, and things looked steadier.

Economic policy was another problem largely overcome by late 1935. While there had been a near-euphoria about Britain's industrial prospects in the aftermath of the 1931 election, ironically, 1932 was to be the worst year of the slump, as the official figure for unemployment rose again to peak at nearly three million by the beginning of 1933. This was embarrassing to the government; however, it could claim that its policies needed time to work, and Labour, which had presided over a more-than-doubling of the figures in a two-year period, was hardly in a position to convince the voters of its ability to do better. By the time another election began to be due, the figures were falling impressively, and the radical proposals of Lloyd George's rather opportunistic 'New Deal' in 1935 could be ignored, though not before the Cabinet had staged a useful public relations stunt in listening patiently to his views. At the time of the 1935 election unemployment stood at 1,595,689 insured workers, a figure lower than at any time since February 1930. In 1934, the cuts of 1931 had been restored; taxes had been cut. If not dynamic, the National Government seemed economically competent; that, in itself, seemed a bonus in comparison with other recent administrations. Thus the government looked a reasonable proposition to most electors.

It might have had less appeal if it had not had the good sense to climb down in the Unemployment Assistance Board (UAB) crisis early in 1935. The government, like its predecessors since the early 1920s, realized that if it was to reject radical initiatives to slash the unemployment figures, it must maintain a reasonable system of relief for the unemployed. The problem was that the system it had inherited was a mess. The unemployment insurance fund, intended to be self-financing, was bankrupt in all but name; the whole administration of the various forms of benefit was chaotic. Into the breach stepped Chamberlain, with the same belief in administrative rationality that was to get him into greater trouble with Hitler later in the decade. The old system would be swept away, and the issue taken out of politics, by the appointment of an independent UAB to replace the local, and often stubbornly independent, Public Assistance Committees. It would set national rates for means-tested benefits to those whose entitlement to insurance benefit had expired. But when the new rates were introduced in January 1935, they were in many cases lower than those that

14

had been paid locally. The result was a great upsurge of popular indignation, encompassing not only the Communist-led National Unemployed Workers' Movement (NUWM), but also the Labour movement, the churches, and a number of Conservative back-benchers who, fearing the loss of their marginal seats, urged the government to think again. After an embarrassing interval in which they tried − contrary to the intention of the legislation − to persuade the UAB to change its mind, the government withdrew the regulations and announced that whichever of the old or new rates of benefit was the higher would apply. On one level this was a humanitarian act; on another, a fairly spineless capitulation. But whatever else it was, it was politic. A potentially disastrous crisis had been circumvented, to the electoral benefit of the government.

Another issue from which the steam had largely gone by the time of the 1935 election was that of India, much to the relief of the Conservative leadership which saw it as one of the greatest dangers to party unity and the survival of the government. Seen by many Tories as the keystone of the Empire, India's form of government had become an increasing cause for concern. Baldwin's basic view was that the liberalization of Britain's rule should be continued because, otherwise, India might divide British politics as bitterly as Ireland had done twenty years earlier. Thus, even before the formation of the National Government, Baldwin had largely followed MacDonald's line. Now the two worked closely together, and the ultimate product was the Government of India Act, 1935, by which responsible government was established in the provinces − a stepping-stone to full responsible government. But this line met strong opposition from Churchill and the Conservative right, who felt that the Indians were not yet fit for self-government and that the break-up of the Empire was being signalled. During the tortuously slow progress of the legislation there were frequent, and serious, Conservative back-bench revolts, but they were never sufficient to defeat the government, and the Bill was passed in July of 1935. Although bitterness remained, especially between Churchill and Sir Samuel Hoare, the India Secretary, the immediate problem was over by the time of

15

the 1935 election: another difficulty had been surmounted just in time.

The same was true, by and large, of foreign policy. Or so it seemed at the time. The government, and Simon in particular, had come in for much criticism for not doing more to promote the success of the World Disarmament Conference at Geneva, but by 1935 Germany was rearming and Italy was invading Abyssina: the focus had shifted. In response, Hoare, now Foreign Secretary, went to Geneva that September to pledge British support for collective economic action against Italian aggression. The League of Nations was popular in Britain: Hoare's action was widely applauded, except by the Labour Party which claimed, somewhat tendentiously, that he had stolen its policy.

Thus the government entered the general election of November 1935 with few fears, especially since its opponents were in such difficulties (see below). The past four years had seen some serious electoral reverses. The loss of the London County Council to Labour in March 1934 was a severe blow, while the period since 1931 had produced some unwelcome by-election results, most notably at East Fulham in October 1933, when an apparently safe seat had fallen to Labour on a swing of 29.1 per cent. After East Fulham, '[t]he spectre of a 1931-scale rout, in reverse, was raised' (Cook and Ramsden (eds), 1973, p. 112). But this was nonsense. The government's electoral base was incredibly strong. Of forty-eight government seats which fell vacant, only nine were lost; the average by-election swing against the government, at 15.8 per cent, though higher than for any government since the war, was still below the 20 per cent Labour would need at a general election to win a bare overall majority of five (Cook and Ramsden (eds), 1973, p. 389; Thorpe, 1991, pp. 270–1). And the odds were moving heavily against Labour by late 1935. Thus it was no surprise that at the 1935 general election the National Government won another comprehensive victory and established itself in power for the remainder of the decade. Problems faced had been overcome, competently if unspectacularly. But it is in

16

the nature of politics that problems tend not to go away for very long.

Almost immediately after the election, in fact, the government was plunged into crisis, and remained in difficulties for the next twelve months. During 1935 it had made moves towards a foreign policy based on collective security through the League of Nations. However, the policy of sanctions against Italy masked severe misgivings about alienating Mussolini at a time when Hitler seemed a more serious threat in Europe, and shortly after the election Hoare met the French Prime Minister, Pierre Laval, in Paris. They agreed to partition Abyssinia, giving the plains to Italy and leaving the emperor, Haile Selassie, with the mountain areas. In *Realpolitik* terms the plan made sense; there was little worth saving in Haile Selassie's regime, and Italy was going to win anyway. The plan avoided the possibility of conflict with Mussolini, and perhaps opened the way to a co-operative stand against Germany. Forty years earlier such a manoeuvre would have aroused scarcely a murmur; now it was a major embarrassment, smacking as it did of secret diplomacy and power politics. It seemed to encapsulate an expediency in policy which was beginning to conflict with the idealistic views of increasing numbers of middle-class people in particular. A public outcry led to Hoare being repudiated by the Cabinet — even though it had agreed to the basic line he had followed — and forced to resign. But he was an able and ambitious man, and his friendship with Beaverbrook meant that ministers preferred to have him in, rather than out, of the Cabinet. Thus he was a cause for concern until his reinstatement to cabinet rank in June 1936. Before then, however, the Colonial Secretary, J. H. Thomas, had also been forced to resign because he had leaked budget secrets. The scandal was well-handled, and there was surprisingly little damage to the government as a whole, but it was another cause for alarm and it is little wonder that the ageing Baldwin suffered a nervous breakdown. Only months after its great victory, the government seemed to be staggering, led by an old, deaf man on the edge of despair.

17

But, of course, the economy continued to prosper; and the next crisis was handled with much greater ease. In January 1936 King George V had died, to be succeeded by his eldest son as Edward VIII. The latter's unstable character and private life (at forty-one he was still unmarried) had long worried many people; politicians were especially concerned by his tendency to make spectacular but often ill-judged comments on the state of the nation. More worrying still was his relationship with a twice-divorced American woman, Wallis Simpson. When he decided that he wanted to marry her after her divorce became absolute in October, a crisis could not be far away. The Church of England, the Dominions, and what was believed to be 'public opinion' were all opposed to the idea of a divorcee becoming Queen. Baldwin, handling the crisis tenaciously and decisively, put the stark choice before Edward. The latter chose marriage to Mrs Simpson, and on 11 December the Abdication Act was passed in a single day. There was little backing for Edward; Churchill's characteristically emotional and ill-considered attempt to rally support for the King further distanced him, not only from other Conservatives, but also from Labourites who wanted to form a concerted attack on the government's foreign policy. Although it would be wrong to attribute overly machiavellian motives to their actions, it seems clear that the government was relieved to be rid of so unsuitable a monarch; his younger brother, who succeeded as George VI, was much more acceptable (and already a family man). Baldwin's handling of the crisis, and, more importantly, the continuing prosperity, meant that he was able to resign in a blaze of glory after the Coronation in May 1937.

Chamberlain was the undisputed successor. He had had to wait a long time for the leadership: at sixty-eight he was not much younger than the man he was replacing. Age had hardened his intolerance of opposition and added to his determination to 'sort things out'. In an increasingly difficult world, there was a lot of work to be done. He also felt the need to make his mark: to prove himself, as his distinguished father and brother had been unable to do. This meant that he would be firm to the point of obstinacy and that relations within the

Conservative Party, and the government as a whole, would deteriorate, although not to the extent that a Labour government ever looked a serious possibility. At the same time, Chamberlain's partisan rhetoric would often arouse hostility, and his inability to resist a telling phrase would deliver a number of hostages to fortune.

By this stage it was more of a Conservative government than ever. The resignation of Thomas (1936) and retirement of MacDonald (1937) had robbed National Labour of any meaning it had had; the Liberal Nationals held their seats on Conservative sufferance, although they still had clout within the government, with Simon succeeding Chamberlain as Chancellor of the Exchequer. But against two National Labourites (in minor positions), and four Liberal Nationals, there were now fifteen Conservatives in the Cabinet.

For obvious reasons, this government's foreign policy ('appeasement') has aroused most interest among historians. It was not a policy of weakness or vacillation; Chamberlain's government was not, on the whole, drifting. The premise was that Hitler, though obnoxious in many ways, was leader of a nation with real grievances stemming from the Versailles peace settlement. Those grievances, if unresolved, might lead to conflict in Europe, a conflict into which Britain would probably be drawn. Yet Britain could not afford to fight a major war; Chamberlain had not worked hard at the Treasury for five and a half years to see Britain's precarious prosperity sacrificed over the squabbles of continental nations. Britain, he believed, should extricate itself from Europe and concentrate on its Empire. Thus the way forward was to 'settle' central Europe by giving in to Hitler's justifiable and limited demands, although prudence dictated British rearmament just in case. This strategy was pursued until Hitler invaded the non-German areas of Czechoslovakia in March 1939; only when it seemed that there could be no final solution which would satisfy Hitler and leave British interests intact, did Chamberlain's policy begin to change. Appeasement produced divisions within the party, but had the support of the majority while it was actively pursued: and at least the delay of British action until September

19

1939 meant that the country went to war reasonably prepared, united, and with the support of the Dominions.

At home, the government continued to pursue limited reforms so long as budgetary stringency, the ideology of the primacy of private enterprise and limited state involvement in society, and the economy allowed them. In 1938 the Holidays with Pay Act increased workers' rights to paid holidays. In the same year coal royalties were nationalized. Unemployment insurance, extended to agricultural workers in 1936, was broadened to some domestic servants. The government continued to give limited assistance to the rationalization of industry but, overall, it tried to maintain the cautious strategy which had evolved in the early 1930s, believing that excessive government intervention would lead to renewed depression. Increasingly, the needs of rearmament and civil defence swallowed up resources, and the government was forced to borrow to pay its way. But this in no way represented a conversion to 'Keynesianism' (see chapter 3).

The later 1930s saw a growth of Conservative dissent in a number of areas. Appeasement led to rifts: Anthony Eden resigned as Foreign Secretary in February 1938 and protested quietly from the back-benches; Alfred Duff Cooper resigned over the Munich agreement that October; others, like Churchill, who had never been in the National Government, were more forthright in their opposition. But they lacked substantial numerical support. Domestic policy also provoked some dissension. Increasingly, younger, progressive Conservatives were irked by the government's pessimism, rigidity, and apparent lack of vision, and felt that more could be done to promote prosperity within a capitalist democracy. Perhaps the leading figure here was Harold Macmillan, whose book *The Middle Way* (1938) advocated more interventionist economic policies, including planning, public works, and the extension of public control, in order to improve living standards. However, Macmillan was a marginal figure in the Conservative Party of the 1930s, and his efforts did little to provoke outright opposition to the government, in part at least because mainstream party policy was continuing to move in a progressive direction, albeit at a slower rate than some of the Young Turks would have liked (Ramsden, 1987). The key point here is that, before the war, in neither foreign nor domestic policy was criticism of the government a threat to its survival.

The state of the Conservative Party itself also caused some concern at this time. The once-excellent organization had become rather rusty, for one thing. The ease with which the 1931 and 1935 elections had been won had bred complacency throughout the party. There was growing concern, too, at the limited social basis of the party in parliament, and at methods of candidate selection. In January 1939 Ian Harvey, a prospective candidate, issued a press statement to the effect that anyone unable to subscribe more than £100 a year to their constituency association had 'hardly any chance at all' of being adopted as a candidate and that the party, for all its talk of 'true democracy' was in fact 'restrict[ing] the representatives of the people by pernicious financial demands' (Ross, 1948, pp. 297−9).

But after almost a decade in power some loss of popularity was to be expected, and what remains impressive is that the government looked likely to win the next general election when it came. Whereas by-elections between 1931 and 1935 had often shown massive swings against the Conservatives, those after the 1935 election, generally, did not. In sixty-four by-elections, Labour made thirteen gains, but only one in a seat it had not held before, and the swings 'were never big enough to suggest an overall Labour majority' (Cook and Ramsden (eds), 1973, p. 116). For all its difficulties, then, Chamberlain's peacetime government, like its National predecessors, was never within measurable distance of losing power.

As we have seen, the National Governments experienced a decade of severe problems. Some of them were self-inflicted − such as the failure to exclude the free-trade Liberals before the 1931 election, or the UAB crisis of 1935 − but others were really beyond the government's power to control. What is perhaps most impressive is that it maintained its fundamental strategy throughout the decade, despite calls for more positive action on unemployment or, later, on rearmament. These governments were pessimistic; if things were bad, they tended to view alternative policies as likely to make matters even worse rather than better. But it was a rough world in which they were working — there were many countries worse off than Britain, economically and/or politically. Answers came more easily in the iconoclastic days of war, or later, sitting in warm university studies of the fifties and sixties and in a world — or at least a Western world — made safe for democracy, and of social welfare politics, mixed economies and prosperity. Today, once again, the world is a more uncertain place: and that enables one the better to see that the National Governments, increasingly Conservative-dominated as the decade wore on, were essentially dull, but competent.

THE LABOUR PARTY AND SOCIALISM

By 1939 Labour had clearly established itself as the only realistic alternative to Conservative government. But that was something of a mixed blessing. While it meant that, in 1945, it was ideally placed to benefit from a tide of anti-Conservatism, there was no such tide in the 1930s, especially since Labour had an uninspiring, functional image in the eyes of those very idealists who would support it by the end of the war (Orwell, 1941, pp. 113–16). Paradoxically, the collapse of the Liberals made Labour's position worse; in the 1920s it had at least been able to win seats by the Liberals splitting its opponents' vote. Now it had to fight its own battles; and in the 1930s, that meant losing them.

Few Labourites would have predicted such an outcome from the perspective of 1929, however. In 1928 Labour, under the leadership of MacDonald, had adopted a new programme, *Labour and the Nation*, on which its 1929 manifesto was based. This was a classic document of the MacDonald Labour Party: plenty of promises but no priorities. Essentially it aimed to increase Labour's vote rather than to provide a blueprint for government. At the 1929 election, despite receiving fewer votes than the Conservatives, Labour took 287 seats to their 260 (the Liberals won 59). For the first time it was the largest

22

party in parliament. A mood of euphoria swept the Labour movement as MacDonald formed his second minority government. But that mood was soon to change. After a bright start, with a string of minor foreign policy successes, the government was hit by economic recession. During its two years in office, the official unemployment level rose from 1.1 million to 2.8 million, and the government was unable even to stem the rising tide. Its 'unqualified pledge' of 1929 'to deal immediately and practically with this question' (Craig, 1975, p. 82) now looked ridiculous: various expedients were suggested, and some were tried, but they achieved little. More radical solutions than those of MacDonald and his colleagues were proposed, most notably by a junior minister, Sir Oswald Mosley, but they were rejected. It used to be argued that this was a tragic mistake, but it is difficult to refute the argument of the Chancellor of the Exchequer, Philip Snowden, that radical departures at such a time would have destroyed international confidence and so made matters even worse (Skidelsky, 1967; McKibbin, 1990, pp. 197–227).

The alternative course was uninspiring, and represented the bankruptcy of gradualist socialism in an economic recession. Believing that socialism could only come from the *success* of capitalism, MacDonald and Snowden had no distinctive policy to deal with capitalism in crisis. The only solutions they had were orthodox ones – reducing taxation and public expenditure, and allowing industry to become more competitive by cutting its costs and, hence, wages. In short, the Labour Party aimed to batten down the hatches and wait for better times to come so that the advance towards socialism could be resumed. But this was bound to bring them into conflict with the left, which would demand more radical policies, and, more importantly, with the trade unions, which aimed to preserve and improve wage levels. Reform, necessarily, had to take a back seat, although there were some advances in housing and transport; again, this annoyed sections of the Labour movement, especially the unions.

By the early summer of 1931 the government faced a series of difficulties which suggested that its days were numbered.

First, the alienation of the left had led to the secession of Mosley and a handful of other Labour MPs to form the New Party. More seriously, the left-wing MPs of the nominally allied Independent Labour Party (ILP) were in a state of permanent rebellion against the government. The trade-union movement was also alienated and increasingly hostile. Important sections of electoral support were antagonized: Jews over the government's policy in Palestine, Catholics over its attitude towards church schools. The morale of the Parliamentary Labour Party (PLP) had collapsed. The Cabinet was full of ageing, tired, and quarrelsome ministers, some of them yearning for retirement or at least for a spell in the — as they thought — calmer waters of opposition. The parliamentary position was turning for the worse as the Liberal Party, on whose sufferance Labour governed, began to break up. And all this was reflected in a dismal run of by-election results, with seats lost and massive swings against Labour.

The way the government fell surprised everyone, however. The budget was in deficit, and the May Committee had been set up in February 1931 to report on means of cutting public expenditure. In July Snowden, who wanted to 'bounce' his colleagues into big cuts, published the committee's report, predicting a £120 million budget deficit, without comment, on the day that parliament rose for the summer recess. The aim was to create a domestic scare which would force the Cabinet's hand; but, coming on top of a European financial crisis and wavering confidence in Britain, the report started a flight from sterling. Ministers were recalled from vacation, and told they had to make cuts. On 21 August, after a series of meetings, the Cabinet agreed to economies of £56 million, made up mainly of cuts in public-sector salaries, despite the declared opposition of the TUC. However, this was well below the £96 million demanded by the May Committee. The opposition leaders, whose support would be necessary to pass the proposals, objected, as did the bankers, particularly since international financial opinion was now seeing a cut in unemployment benefit as the acid test of Britain's commitment to 'sound finance'. On 23 August the Cabinet voted eleven to nine in favour of a 10 per cent cut in benefit, but the minority, which included the Foreign Secretary and party General Secretary, Arthur Henderson, was so large and important that MacDonald was forced to tender his government's resignation.

The following day MacDonald formed the National Government. He took Snowden, Thomas and a few others with him, but the bulk of the Labour Party moved into opposition. At first there were signs of euphoria, but these soon passed, and by the time the election campaign started six weeks later Labour headquarters was expecting the loss of up to a hundred seats. A number of factors accounted for this change. The first was the uninspiring performance of Henderson, elected against his wishes as party leader. A moderate, he was keen to keep the way open for MacDonald's return, and in any case to minimize any swing to the left. But these tactics bemused and ultimately demoralized many Labourites. Secondly, the gradual revelation of the extent to which the ex-ministers had been prepared to countenance cuts sobered many. Thirdly, the success of the National Government in passing the cuts, and in retaining its coherence long enough to make a united appeal to the country, disappointed hopes that it would prove an unworkable and ridiculous body. Insofar as the government's continuation meant the maximization of straight fights against Labour candidates, it became clear that Labour's position was dire indeed, since many MPs owed victory in 1929 to a split opposition vote: now they would need not only to keep their previous support, but to pick up new votes just to retain their seats. Finally, the party was ill-prepared organizationally for an election. For example, most of the party's standard literature was useless because it carried MacDonald's portrait. All this led to a gradual divorce from reality, and the party entered the campaign with an ill-thought-out, radical manifesto in which few of its leaders seriously believed.

The election campaign itself was a disaster for Labour. The party was pilloried over the performance of the second Labour government, especially over unemployment; the ex-ministers were, not unjustly, exposed for their conduct in August; and the issues on which Labour had hoped to capitalize, such as opposition to cuts and tariffs, did little to help the party, partly because both expedients had been considered by the Cabinet in August, and partly because the government was able to make out a convincing case for both. There were scares and stunts, but they were mere froth for the government, and in any case these tactics were not confined to one side. By the last weekend of the campaign Labour's leaders were more convinced than ever that they would lose; and the results themselves were disastrous. Labour needed a considerable increase in its vote merely to retain the seats it had. Instead, its vote fell by about a quarter, and in terms of seats things were even worse. Only forty-six Labour MPs were returned; of the late Cabinet only George Lansbury kept his seat, and he became Chairman of the Parliamentary Labour Party while Henderson remained, officially, leader.

Over the next two years Labour swung even further to the left. At first, there were three basic views on the line that Labour should take. The first was that of Henderson – that there should be no impulsive changes and that 1931 should be written off as an aberration, a defeat due solely to special causes which would not prevail in a future contest. Labour should stick to its 1928 programme and wait for the tide of 'gradualism' to return. This line, though, was unconvincing to most sections of the movement, and Henderson's resignation of the party leadership in October 1932 was a recognition of its failure. Secondly, the leading lights on the General Council of TUC, especially men like Ernest Bevin (General Secretary of the Transport and General Workers' Union) and Walter Citrine (TUC Gerenal Secretary) as well as the more hard-headed Labour politicians, like Hugh Dalton, argued that Labour could still work towards the gradual implementation of socialist policies. However, MacDonald's failure showed the need for the policies to be better worked-out and prioritized. This line was pushed by the TUC and particularly by the National Joint Council (National Council of Labour from 1934), the union-dominated body reconstituted after the 1931 election, which played an increasingly central role in defining the party's outlook as the decade wore on. But it was the third,

26

left, argument which seemed to be carrying all before it in 1931−3. This held that 1931 had been the inevitable result of trying to reach an accommodation with capitalism; that there could be no such accommodation; that rising unemployment signalled the impending collapse of capitalism; and that therefore, Labour should adopt radical socialist policies and prepare to implement them rapidly on its return to power. This line held sway in the PLP, besieged as it was in the Commons by Conservatives; it was also the line of the ILP and, after it left Labour in 1932, of the Socialist League, the body set up to replace it as a left-wing ginger group.

A number of factors accounted for the party's initial swing to the left. First, the resumption and intensification of the increase in unemployment from early 1932 suggested that capitalism was in its death-throes. The old MacDonaldite belief in socialism emerging painlessly from the success of capitalism now seemed nonsensical: indeed, the march of Fascism on the Continent, and the formation of the British Union of Fascists in 1932, both seemed to suggest that an apocalyptic struggle was at hand. Secondly, recent memories of 1931 were bitter; it seemed that any Labour government which tried to accommodate itself to capitalism, instead of challenging it head-on, would be doomed to failure, if only − it was felt − because of the apparent power of financial institutions to sabotage its efforts. Thirdly, the Labour left was helped immeasurably by the ILP's decision to leave the party in 1932. It had been possible for moderate leaders to deal with the ILP on a managerial basis − that is, to marginalize it by pointing to its disloyalty rather than challenging its arguments intellectually. The Socialist League, which replaced the ILP, was at first less tightly structured: its arguments had to be met, and that posed real problems for the party leadership. Fourthly, there was a lack of real resistance at this stage. Many moderate leaders (not just MacDonald and his cohorts) had been swept away in 1931; most had lost their seats in parliament, and became preoccupied with other things. Henderson, for example, was busy presiding over the World Disarmament Conference at Geneva. The mantle of parliamentary leadership moved left-

27

wards, to Lansbury and his assistants, Clement Attlee and Sir Stafford Cripps. In addition, the trade union leaders were too busy trying to shore up their crumbling membership and to resist wage cuts in large areas of industry to take a lead in party matters. For the time being they were prepared, albeit grudgingly, to let the left have its head. The symbolic high-water mark of the swing to the left was the adoption of a resolution at the party's conference at Hastings in October 1933 that, in the event of war, the Labour movement would initiate a general strike to prevent Britain's participation.

By 1935, however, things seemed to have changed quite considerably. Again, no single factor was decisive. The economy began to recover in the last quarter of 1932, and unemployment was falling from early 1933 onwards. The argument that socialism could come from the workings of a successful capitalism became sustainable once again. Secondly, the increasing stridency and organization of the Socialist League, and the growing unpopularity of its wealthy leading figure, Cripps, began to act as a block to the left. It is worth bearing in mind the irony by which the left swept all before it at the 1932 party conference, when the League was hardly formed, whereas, two years later, all seventy-five of its carefully planned amendments to the new party programme were defeated. In addition, the Communist Party's change of line in 1933, by which it stopped denouncing Labour as 'social fascist' and began once again to campaign for a united front, was counterproductive in that it immediately made most Labourites more, rather than less, suspicious of the far left. Thirdly, rising employment created an easier atmosphere, which meant that trade unionists could spend more time on the party. Fourthly, concrete policies began to emerge from the party's centre and right as those committees set up to study future policy in the aftermath of 1931 began to report. The committees' findings were embodied in *For Socialism and Peace* (1934), the first thorough-going Labour programme since 1928. It was 'more socialist in tone than *Labour and the Nation* and includ[ed] more precise and extensive proposals for nationalisation', but it 'scarcely represented a revolution in Labour's economic thinking' (Pimlott,

28

1977, p. 38). The move was not so much towards more radical policies as towards a clearer delineation of how the old policies would be implemented. Fifthly, Labour's victory in the London County Council elections of March 1934, whereby it took control of the capital for the first time, was won under the impeccably moderate leadership of Herbert Morrison; this merely confirmed the trend towards more 'saleable policies' which was in any case probable due to the proximity of the next general election. Finally, foreign developments, particularly the rise of Hitler in Germany and his consequent destruction of free trade unionism, and, in 1935, Italian aggression in Abyssinia, discredited the left's argument that there was nothing to choose between the 'capitalist' powers, and that pacifism was a viable option.

One direct casualty of the shift to the right was the leader. In the immediate aftermath of 1931, Lansbury's inspirational leadership and fundamentalist socialism had made him a good leader for a demoralized party. But by 1935 his pacifism, vagueness, and leftism meant that he came increasingly into conflict with the hard-headed figures like Bevin and Dalton who were beginning to dominate the party. At the party conference, shortly before the election campaign began, the party voted overwhelmingly for sanctions against Italy in response to its invasion of Abyssinia. Lansbury saw this as a hostile act which might lead to war, and, as a pacifist, opposed it. He was overwhelmingly defeated, and, in poor health anyway, he resigned. Attlee, his deputy, succeeded him on a temporary basis.

The general election of November 1935 found Labour in grave difficulties. The 1931 defeat had left it in very weak position: it was unlikely to make very extensive gains, particularly since the virtual collapse of the Liberal Party meant that most of its candidates faced straight fights against the Nationals. Its leadership lacked experience at a time when domestic and international problems seemed to demand that very quality. Its policy, though better worked-out than ever before, was seen as too radical and class-oriented at a time when the country seemed to be moving towards increasing

29

prosperity under a competent, if uninspiring, government. The record of the second Labour government was still a potent cry against the party — for all the later condemnations of the National Governments, it was Labour which had the image of the party of depression and incompetence in the 1930s. And the gradual resolution of most of its problems by the National Government meant there were few openings for Labour attack; in particular, Hoare's espousal of collective security satisfied many voters' more moralistic aspirations. In these circumstances, Labour did not expect victory in November 1935: party headquarters was reported as expecting a government majority of 113 (Stannage, 1980, p. 150). Even so, to win only 154 seats (with a slightly higher share of the votes than in 1929) was a disappointment. Particularly worrying was the patchiness of its performance: in many areas, especially Lancashire and the west Midlands, a great deal would still have to be done. Labour was still not appealing widely outside the more unionized sections of the industrial working class.

Following its defeat, the party's first task was to elect a leader. Many of the more prominent members were now MPs again. However, Attlee beat off the challenge of Morrison and Arthur Greenwood, and was to remain party leader until 1955. This decision baffled some and infuriated others: Dalton, who had campaigned hard for Morrison, called it 'a wretched, disheartening result' (Pimlott (ed), 1986, p. 196). Although Attlee had some positive attributes, and benefited from the loyalty of members of the late parliament who had come to have a high regard for his abilities, it seems likely that he won largely by default. Greenwood was distrusted as a heavy drinker and a freemason, and had made little impact in the 1931—5 parliament despite having been re-elected at a by-election in 1932. Morrison was considered too much of a Londoner, was still seen as a MacDonaldite who had almost joined the National Government in 1931, was not popular with trade unionists (particularly Bevin), and was expected to be a 'strong' leader in the mode of MacDonald at a time when such an idea was anathema. In addition, there might have been misgivings, given the circumstances surrounding Lansbury's departure,

30

as to whether a man who had been a conscientious objector in the First World War would be 'sound' enough on defence and foreign policy. Attlee won at least as much because of who he was *not*, as because of who he *was*; and his later success should not obscure the fact that he was a largely ineffectual leader during the 1930s, often conspired against, sometimes ill (which meant he was out of action for most of 1939), and occasionally ignored by the people who really mattered.

The policy over which Attlee presided moved back towards gradualism during these years: gradualism refined, but gradualism nonetheless. In 1937 the party adopted *Labour's Immediate Programme*, which represented a recognition of the failures of previous documents by prioritizing policies in terms of what could be achieved within a single five-year period of office. The Bank of England would be nationalized, but the proposal to do the same with the joint stock banks was quietly forgotten. Railways and fuel and power would also be taken into the public sector. There was a greater emphasis on planning, especially in the location of industry – a development of the government's existing regional policy. The school-leaving age would be raised to sixteen, the means test would be abolished, and pensions, workmen's compensation and health services would all be improved. It would be going too far to say that all was now well. A great deal remained to be done: as the National Executive Committee (NEC) was told in 1940, many of its policy statements had not been updated for some years. But gone was the apocalyptic language of the 1931 manifesto; gone was the catch-all approach of *Labour and the Nation*. In their place was a hard-headed programme which was to help form the basis of the work of the post-war Labour governments. The left had been defeated.

Why was this? The economic situation certainly played a large part. Although the economy moved into recession late in 1937, the rapid recovery, due largely to government expenditure on rearmament, suggested that state intervention could negate the adverse workings of the trade cycle, as Keynes argued. Indeed, Keynesianism became increasingly respectable within the Labour Party at this time, a fact which is in itself

31

instructive, given that Keynes's aim was to bolster, rather than to overthrow, capitalism. The idea that socialism would evolve from a successful capitalism was now back centre-stage, as E. F. M. Durbin's *The Politics of Democratic Socialism* (1940), written during 1939, made clear. In a sense — although no one would have admitted it — this was refined MacDonaldism. Secondly, Labour felt the need to attract the political 'middle ground' from the government. To that end it also refused to co-operate with Communists, or to become involved in extra-parliamentary action for the unemployed or against fascism. Communist calls for 'united' or 'popular fronts' were met with a solid refusal from the party leadership, backed by repeated annual conference votes. However, the party also refused to act with other parties; in January 1939 Cripps was expelled for going against this line. The leadership argued that such co-operation would be a distraction and that Labour could win the next election on its own. In fact, it was unlikely to do so, but the NEC was probably right in arguing that participation in things like the 'National Opposition', mooted in late 1938, would do the party no good, and probably some damage. Thirdly, the Socialist League continued to marginalize itself, allowing party leaders to ignore its arguments and instead focus on the managerial aspect until, in 1937, it was forced to disband, having repeated the ILP's mistakes. Finally, the growing threat of the Fascist powers led more and more Labourites towards support for rearmament and, if necessary, armed struggle; in 1937 the PLP abstained in the vote on the defence estimates, rather than, as in previous years, voting against — a major symbolic change since the 'pacifist' resolution of 1933. The international, no less than the domestic, realities had moved Labour to the right.

That said, there was little indication that Labour would have improved its parliamentary position appreciably at the general election due by the end of 1940. At municipal and by-elections Labour continued to mop up the losses of 1931, but that was all. There were no major advances into new territory. In 1937, G. D. H. Cole had shown that to win a bare overall majority Labour would need to hold all its existing seats and take all those where the government's majority was under 6,000. Cole was right to say that it was 'a ridiculous supposition' to believe that this could be achieved at the next election (1937, pp. 272–3). Indeed, the special circumstances of 1939 – the row over Cripps, Attlee's illness, and so on – made short-term prospects worse, not better. The Second World War was to make Labour capable of winning majorities in parliament. Before then, for all their anxieties, the National Governments were safely esconced in power.

The 1930s, then, posed great difficulties for the Labour Party. Its period in office saw it with no idea of how to cope with a multitude of problems. The long-standing belief that socialism was the inevitable end-product of an increasingly prosperous capitalism seemed to be discredited as capitalism became patently less prosperous. The result of this, and the calamitous events of 1931, was a temporary, and in some ways illusory, swing to the left. But the preference of the majority of the party for a more accommodating stance *vis-á-vis* the existing order soon became apparent, and as the economy began once again to prosper, so once again moderate policies returned, albeit better worked-out and prioritized than ever before. The left did not help itself but the process was not determined by its actions. By 1939 some problems had been resolved, and any lingering doubts about Labour being the only viable alternative to the Conservatives had been assuaged, but others remained. It was to be the Second World War which solved the party's problems of credibility, policy, and leadership. When that war broke out, Labour was still a long way from power.

THE LIBERALS

The 1930s saw the demise of the Liberal Party as a serious force in British politics. It had been in decay for many years; now it crashed into the near-irrelevance it was to endure until the 1960s. Never really reunited after the split of 1916, when one Liberal, H. H. Asquith, was replaced by another, David

33

Lloyd George, as Prime Minister, it now found itself squeezed out by the moderation of the National Governments and the growing realism of Labour. It must be added, though, that it did little to prevent this.

In 1926, Asquith had finally retired as leader and been succeeded by Lloyd George, who had eventually returned to the party after his six years as Prime Minister of the predominantly Conservative Coalition Government (1916–22). Between 1926 and the 1929 election, Lloyd George spent prodigious amounts of his personal political fund on revitalizing the party organization and developing a new programme. In real terms it was perhaps the most expensive campaign ever waged by a British political party (Pinto-Duschinsky, 1981, p. 91). For the first time in years the party appeared relatively united. Constituency organizations were revived. The policy proposals of the *Yellow Book*, worked out by a committee of prominent Liberals including economists like Keynes and H. D. Henderson, were exciting if not, to many observers, terribly convincing, claiming as they did that loan-financed public works could reduce unemployment substantially.

Even so, the results of the 1929 election were disappointing for the party. Although it should be remembered that no senior Liberal seriously expected to win, obtaining less than a quarter of the votes and, worse, only fifty-nine seats, was a disappointment. In too many seats they were clearly the third party, with voters realizing that a vote for the Liberals was a vote wasted. Even so, the inconclusive nature of the result meant that Lloyd George was in a potentially strong position. His aim had been to win enough seats to form a Liberal bloc which could then use its influence to bargain with the two main parties over policies and, perhaps, places in government. This did not happen. Baldwin, who had a hearty dislike of Lloyd George, Liberal policy, and three-party politics, refused to bargain with the former premier, who was thus forced into the somewhat unwilling arms of MacDonald and Labour. The Liberal Parliamentary Party (LPP) was also too fractious a body to act as a coherent bloc, shifting its allegiance at the whim of a leader whom many of its members distrusted thoroughly. The 1929

34

result, in addition, left the party in a very weak position for the future. Labour would retreat, and the Conservatives advance, the longer Labour was in office; yet the Liberals were second in very few Labour seats, while their gains in 1929 had been largely at the expense of a Conservative Party in temporary difficulties.

During the two years of the 1929 parliament, Lloyd George did his best to influence Labour. But it was to little avail. All too often the party, instead of acting as a unit, split three ways in parliamentary divisions: clearly it was breaking up. Straight after the election one Liberal MP joined the Labour Party; by the end of 1930 another group, loosely ranged around Sir John Simon, was negotiating closer co-operation with the Conservatives. In June 1931 he and two others formally resigned the Liberal whip.

The party was in chaos in other ways, too. Its organization virtually collapsed when Lloyd George withdrew his financial support in 1930. By the middle of that year 300 candidates looked like being the maximum number that would be run at the next election, assuming that the men and women could be found. In his darker moments the Liberal Chairman, Ramsay Muir, mentioned the figure of 200. Neither would have been sufficient to convince voters that the party was still a serious electoral force — 308 MPs were required to obtain even a bare majority. Short of electoral reform — which the Labour government was unwilling to concede except on very unfavourable terms, and which would in any case have been rejected by the Conservative majority in the House of Lords — there seemed little way out for the party.

Policy also languished. The promises of 1929 seemed rash rather than bold once the economy moved into headlong depression late that year. Most Liberals had had their doubts about the *Yellow Book* programme — now it seemed that the need was not for more expenditure, but for less. Retrenchment became the watchword; by mid-1930 most Liberals were calling for cuts in state expenditure as the way out of the crisis, while clinging with increasing desperation to the nostrum of free trade. But free trade itself seemed outmoded in a protectionist

35

world. Even Liberals began to doubt its efficacy. By early 1931 Liberals as different as Keynes and E. D. Simon on the left and Sir John Simon on the right had come out for tariffs. Lloyd George and a few of his supporters continued to refer to the *Yellow Book*, but they were fighting a losing battle.

By mid-1931, then, the Liberals were under severe stress, and the events of the latter half of the year merely added to their discomfiture. Serious illness meant that Lloyd George was unable to participate in the August crisis, and his deputy, Sir Herbert Samuel, though experienced, was neither inspiring nor particularly effective. Samuel agreed that large spending cuts were necessary, and realized that his party would never follow him if he tried to buttress Labour. So he allied with the Conservatives in urging economy, and when the National Government was formed he entered the Cabinet and brought his party with him.

At first things went well for the Liberals in the National Government. But once the economies were introduced, the consensus with the Conservatives ended. The latter had been campaigning for tariffs; they would not be put off an early election. Samuel opposed an election because it would clear the way for protection, and also because it would give the Tories a majority in parliament. The National Government might remain in being but the Conservatives would, he believed, be in a position to dictate policy. Also, the Liberals would no longer hold even a notional balance of power. Backed by Lloyd George, Samuel fought a stern rearguard action, but the Conservatives were keen to be rid of him and, to stay in office, he had no alternative but to accept an early election. Even this could not stop about half the LPP abandoning him for the Liberal National Group under Sir John Simon shortly before the election campaign began. But Samuel's decision disgusted Lloyd George, who refused to have anything to do with the official Liberal campaign and, after the election, consituted himself and a motley band of parliamentary relatives as the 'Lloyd George family group'. In reality, Samuel had had little choice. He believed Labour had swung dangerously to the left, and the existence of the Simonites meant that, if he

36

had resigned, his supporters would have been replaced by other Liberals, who might then have taken most of 'middle' Liberal opinion – which supported the government – with them. Resignation would also have ruled out any real prospect of reunion with the Simonites.

This meant that the party was in a very unhappy position in the 1931 election. It made what it could of the 'free hand', but by definition that ruled out a trenchant defence of free trade, which was rapidly becoming the sole litmus test of official Liberalism. The party's candidates were in an equally weak position, especially as the Conservatives, expecting them to leave the government before very long, felt few qualms about opposing them in their constituencies – Samuel was one MP who faced such opposition. At least the National Government umbrella meant that fewer Liberal candidates needed to be run, and in the event only 111 Samuelites came forward. They won thirty-three seats, but Labour was second in most of these, which suggested that a Labour revival might sweep many of them away. In addition, the Liberal share of the vote fell catastrophically – by almost a quarter – in those seats where they faced Labour and Conservative opposition in both 1931 and 1929. The Liberal Nationals might be derided as puppets of the Tories, but at least they won thirty-five seats and began to look like the future of what remained of British Liberalism.

After the election the Liberals' problems multiplied. The conflict over trade policy was only resolved by the notorious 'agreement to differ' (see above) and by the time of the Ottawa agreements there was widespread Liberal feeling that the party's ministers should resign. In September 1932 Samuel and Sir Archibald Sinclair left the Cabinet; but the party did not move into opposition. It was still felt that the National Government was necessary, especially given the important international issues that had to be faced, such as disarmament and India, and also because of the stridency of Labour's opposition. It was only in November 1933, following shrill demands from the grass-roots, that the party found a pretext to move to the opposition benches.

This delay has been seen as damaging, but the party fared no better after the move, and Samuel had had good reason to procrastinate, for his aim was still Liberal reunion. Immediately after the 1931 election he had sounded out Sir John Simon on the possibilities of closer co-operation, but had got nowhere. The Liberal Nationals accepted tariffs and the Ottawa agreements with little demur. In reality, they had no intention of reuniting with the official Liberal Party. The National Government gave men like Simon and Runciman office, in which they could not only satisfy ambition, but also try to uphold Liberal values from within government. The Liberal Party offered only dissension, decline, and decay. In July 1932, a new Liberal National Council had seen formed, and February 1933 had seen the first direct clash between the two groups at the East Fife by-election. By November 1933 even Samuel had to accept that reunion was unlikely; the Liberal Nationals remained in the government throughout the decade. Ultimately they were to unite with the Conservative Party.

Lloyd George remained elusive, too. During the early 1930s he was an enigmatic figure, farming and writing his *War Memoirs*, but always preserving an air of mystery about his political intentions. When he did return to active politics, it was not, as some Liberals had hoped, as the head of the party, but in an independent role. Early in 1935, copying Roosevelt in the USA, he launched his 'New Deal', a final effort to attract political attention. It made little impact, though, and his attempt to use the 'Council of Action' to pinpoint 'progressive' candidates worthy of support at that year's general election was another non-event. In any case, he was now seventy-two, and he spent the rest of the decade farming, writing for newspapers, and making the odd appearance on big parliamentary occasions. Some questioned his judgement when he visited Hitler in 1936, and later, in 1939−40, when he came out as an advocate of a compromise peace. Lloyd George's day had long since passed; by the thirties he was no great loss to the Liberals or anyone else.

Meanwhile the party continued to decay. Organization crumbled further, as the last few agents were sacked and the party's remaining wealthy benefactors continued to die off. By-elections went unfought with monotonous regularity, which was probably as well, since where they were contested the results were usually disastrous. In March 1934 the Liberals lost their last remaining seats on the London County Council. Liberal MPs continued to trickle over to Labour and the Liberal Nationals. In November 1933 a 'demob happy' Muir, now Chairman of the National Liberal Federation, had spoken boldly of fighting 400 seats at the next general election, but a year later he took 'a gloomy, almost despairing, view of [Liberal] prospects' (Stannage, 1980, p. 103). It was hardly surprising that Muir expected a dismal performance at the 1935 election, and in this he was proved right. The Liberals could put up only 161 candidates and so, unlike the government and Labour, their manifesto could not ask for office, still less power, but merely 'an effective representation of Liberal opinion' in the new House of Commons (Craig, 1975, p. 111). Only 21 Liberals were elected; each candidate obtained, on average, only 13 per cent of the votes cast (Cook, 1976, p. 122). The party's overall share of the poll was a mere 6.7 per cent. Many of the leaders, including Samuel, lost their seats. No area of the country could be called a Liberal stronghold.

This set the scene for the rest of the decade. Indeed, the Liberals were now totally on the fringe of British politics, fighting few by-elections, usually faring badly when they did, and regularly losing seats in local elections. Many of their voters, remnants of the glorious days of old, were dying; and they were not being replaced from among young voters coming on to the register for whom the Liberals had never been anything more than a faction-ridden, impotent, and perhaps rather silly band of people who could not decide which side they were on in the great two-party battle. It is difficult to gainsay Muir, who had written privately in 1934 that it seemed 'highly probable that, as an effective political force, the Liberal Party [was] all-but extinct' (Freeden, 1986, p. 350). By 1938 'the party scarcely functioned in the House of Commons' (Cowling, 1976, p. 233).

It was not even as though they were a powerhouse of ideas.

The Liberal Summer School, which had provided new ideas in the 1920s, had by the early 1930s degenerated into 'an uninspired meeting of speech-makers, almost devoid of controversy and debate, a place where party stalwarts could go for a week's rest and listen politely to addresses from the podium' (Freeden, 1986, p. 337). Some Liberals were involved in various planning movements, like The Next Five Years and Political and Economic Planning, but they hardly spoke for their party. Many Liberals continued to cling to the outdated precepts of a bygone age. There was some realization that free trade had lost the argument with protection, at least for the present; and Sinclair, who succeeded Samuel as leader in 1935, tried to shift the emphasis from free trade to 'freedom'. Could freedom be secured without equality? Muir thought so; many others, like E. D. Simon, thought not. But Simon was swimming against the tide of a party leadership which continued to see its main opponent as socialism, and was forced to join the Labour Party. This, though, raised an awkward question: if primarily anti-socialist, why did Liberals not become Liberal Nationals? There were, of course, ideas coming from people like Keynes and, a little outside our period, William Beveridge. But they were only Liberal by a fairly loose definition of the term. Beveridge did not join the party until after his report on *Social Insurance and Allied Services* was published in 1942, while Keynes was not, by this time, a 'regular' Liberal.

Even as the 1930s began, the Liberals had been in severe difficulties. But few Liberals could perhaps have expected to descend so far during the decade that followed. It was symbolic that, when Churchill formed his Coalition Government in May 1940, there was no Liberal in the five-man War Cabinet; Sinclair had to make do with the post of Air Secretary. It was even more symbolic that the fact aroused little, if any, surprise. For by 1940, after a decade of splits, defeats, and demises, the Liberal Party had all but ceased to exist as a serious force. It had been unable to find any centre ground which the National Government could not occupy with almost equal ease; it had been unable to show that it was radical, and Labour's growing moderation as the decade wore on merely worsened its plight. By 1940 there were still Liberals in Britain; there was still a Liberal Party. But the party had little real existence: it was an amalgam of people too old to change their habits and people with so little in common, politically, as to be at breaking point. It certainly could not inspire middle-class radical idealists. By then, Liberals were Liberals through historical accident or a quirk of fate; few, perhaps, would have rejoined the party, given a fresh start. And no one said that if the nineteenth century had not created the Liberal Party, it would have been necessary to have invented it. There was no Liberal alternative in the 1930s.

THE COMMUNISTS

If the Liberal decline made the re-emergence of two-party politics likely, the failure of the extremes made their continuation largely inevitable. The failure was represented on the left by the Communist Party of Great Britain (CPGB). It had been formed in August 1920, at a time of trade union militancy and, in Russia, confidence about the rapid spread of the revolution across Europe. But within months the militancy had been neutered by economic recession, and the Soviet regime had turned from revolutionary assault to consolidation of the revolution within its own borders. The Communists in Britain had, therefore, to tread a careful path, and pursued a 'united front' policy of seeking to work through the Labour Party. However, all requests for affiliation to that party were rejected, and by the middle of the decade Labour's moderate leaders, who had no time for the Communists whatsoever, had succeeded in first marginalizing and then expelling them from Labour's ranks. The decade ended with the CPGB turning towards a 'class against class' line whereby it claimed that it was the only working-class party, all others being regarded as effectively fascist. This line has often been viewed as a failure, for by November 1930 membership, at 2,555, was only half what it had been at the party's formation (Pelling, 1958, p. 192). By contrast, the 1930s have been called the 'Red Decade'. Not only did party membership increase to 18,000 by 1939; Communism has also been seen as having widespread influence, in, for example, rallying opposition to Fascism and campaigning for the unemployed, so that by 1939 the Communist Party had 'political and social influence [which] was considerably greater than [the] figures would immediately suggest' (Saville, 1988, p. 62). However, Pelling has portrayed a 'Stalinist leadership' under 'an almost slavish subservience to Moscow', making little real impact (1958, pp. 53–4); and, more recently, Harmer has suggested that the period held nothing but disappointment for the party (1988).

The CPGB was something of an artificial creation. There was a Marxist tradition of sorts in Britain, but the groups which drew on it were very heterogeneous until Lenin, with his vast prestige as a successful revolutionary, was able to force most of them together in 1920. The party was affiliated to the Moscow-based Communist International (CI) which, certainly by the later 1920s, was firmly under the control of the Soviet government. The weakness of the Marxist influence in Britain, by comparison with that in Germany, for example, and the numerical and financial weaknesses of the British party made it highly susceptible to Soviet control. Few Communist Parties were as slavish as the CPGB in following the tortuous changes of the Moscow line. This in turn alienated xenophobic British workers, and discredited the party still further in the eyes of much of the mainstream Labour movement.

By late 1927 the CI line was changing to 'class against class' in order to reflect the ultra-left policies of industrialization and collectivization on which the Soviets were about to embark. This not without some opposition in Britain, but it had the support of younger men like the theorist Rajani Palme Dutt, the trade unionist Harry Pollitt, and William Rust of the Young Communist League. Doubtless ambition, loyalty to Moscow, and a desire to be rid of the old, unimaginative, and discredited leadership played a part in their thinking; but there was also a great deal of logic in the British Communist Party's change of line. For one thing, the tactic of trying to affiliate to the Labour Party and then influence it into revolutionary ways had never been very popular within the CPGB. Communists were in the CPGB in the first place because they disliked the Labour Party. Secondly, the united front line had hardly been a success, as the patent failure of the left to radicalize the TUC during the General Strike of 1926 had shown. Thirdly, the Labour Party and the unions were succeeding in eliminating the remaining Communist influence within the Labour movement. By 1928 the National Left-Wing Movement, where Communists co-operated with Labour leftwing activists, was being exterminated by the Labour bureaucracy, and Communist influence in the unions was waning: Pollitt himself was under siege in the Boilermakers' Society. In a sense, the Communists had nowhere else to go but to an anti-Labour line. And, finally, there was soon a sharp downturn in the economy which suggested to many that the apocalyptic collapse of capitalism was at hand. 'Class against class', then, made a lot of sense in the British context: and this was merely reinforced once the second Labour government began to discredit 'reformism' by presiding over massive increases in unemployment, wage cuts, and threats to state benefit levels.

Yet the new line was not a success. Its failure can be overstated: membership fell, but this had been falling dramatically *before* the full adoption of 'class against class', and the decline from 1929 was probably due as much to the economic circumstances of individual Communists as to any other factor. Of greater significance is the trebling of membership in the fourteen months between November 1930 and January 1932, coinciding with the continuation of the slump and the ignominious performance of the Labour Party over that period. But the party's candidates fared disastrously at the 1931 general election (most losing their deposits), and in other areas too the line was not well received. In industry, for example, Communists were urged to stop working through the existing 'reformist' unions and to set up their own unions instead. Only two were formed; neither was a success, and in early 1932 Moscow agreed to the party's request that it be allowed to resume working through the established unions.

The party line was changed more broadly over the next

three years. During 1932 there was a renewed but largely abortive effort to appeal to the rank-and-file of other working-class parties, over the heads of their leaders, by means of the 'united front from below' tactic. Then, with the Nazi takeover in Germany in January 1933, there was further relaxation of 'class against class' with Moscow permitting limited and qualified approaches to the leaders of Labour and the ILP for united action. As expected, Labour gave the Communists short shrift, but there was some co-operation with the ILP. However, the CPGB's aim was clearly to 'asset-strip' the declining party, and by late 1934 it was virtually moribund as a result of 'co-operation'. Even ILP members realized this, and relations cooled considerably; to the Labour leadership, it was still further proof that they should have nothing to do with the Communists.

The rise of the British Union of Fascists during the first half of 1934, and the Communists' prominent role in combating it, helped the party's fortunes, but it was due to the CI's adoption of the 'popular front' strategy in August 1935 that the CPGB began seriously to expand. The new line was introduced because Moscow realized that with the consolidation of the Nazi regime, and its continuing hostility towards the USSR, the latter needed Western allies. In Britain, this strategy of seeking the unity of anti-Fascist forces was directed towards all opponents of the National Government, even Liberals. As a sign of good will, and doubtless with the disasters of 1931 in mind, the party withdrew all but two of its candidates (one of whom, William Gallacher, was elected MP for West Fife) at the 1935 election. But an application for affiliation to the Labour Party was again rejected. However, the crises of the next three years meant that the call for unity was never silenced for long: all such appeals were rejected by Labour, but the popular front period saw CPGB membership expand to 18,000 on the eve of war.

The outbreak of war brought a fresh crisis. The party's leaders had taken the line that the Nazi-Soviet Non-aggression Pact (August 1939) marked no great departure in Soviet policy and that it was just an insurance policy pending an alliance

44

with the Western powers. Pollitt, the party's General Secretary, wrote a pamphlet called *How To Win The War*, which was published on 14 September. It stated unequivocally that '[t]he Communist Party supports the war, believing it to be a just war which should be supported by the whole working class and all friends of democracy' (Dewar, 1976, p. 129). Others, however, like Palme Dutt, the chief ideologue, were less convinced; and he was proved right when, on 28 September, the Soviet Union and Germany made a joint declaration of neutrality. Pollitt was forced to apologize for his 'error' and (temporarily) deposed as General Secretary. Then, on 7 October, the party paper, the *Daily Worker*, which a month earlier had been taking Pollitt's line, stated without a blush: 'This war is not a war for democracy against fascism. It is not a war for the defence of peace against aggression' (Dewar, 1976, p. 131). Palme Dutt declared it a war between socialism and British imperialism. This was to remain the line until June 1941, when the German attack on the USSR once again transformed it into a 'just' war.

Whether this change of line led to a collapse in membership, as is usually claimed, is debatable. Certainly, in the first year of the war, there were anti-war elements to whom the new line would have appealed, and it may be that party membership increased in net terms, even if there was a high turnover (Branson, 1985, p. 271). However, the party was now more marginalized: fellow-travellers like John Strachey, who during the 1930s had been the foremost advocate of the Communist cause in numerous publications, left at this point. So, regardless of membership, influence collapsed. It was not until perceptions were changed by USSR's heroic resistance to the German attack that the party's influence could grow again.

Ostensibly, then, the 1930s were a barren time for the Communists. Membership never exceeded 20,000, and at times it was little more than a tenth of that figure. Yet in many areas, Saville argues, the CPGB did make a significant difference (1988). Work in the unions was one such area. During the 1920s the party had built up a not insignificant role within the unions through its satellite, the National Minority Movement (NMM). By 1928, though, unions were increasingly wary of the NMM; some had prohibited its members from standing for office (Branson, 1985, p. 14). Thus there had been a degree of logic in trying to form separate Communist unions during the 'class against class' phase. But only two emerged, and one of the party's leading trade unionists, Arthur Horner of the South Wales Miners' Federation, staunchly refused to abandon his work there. By early 1932, with Moscow's approval, the party had returned to Horner's line.

The rest of the decade saw increasing Communist influence in some established unions, but it was very patchy. London was the most profitable area of expansion; busworkers in the Transport and General Workers' Union were especially enthusiastic, but that union's leadership largely contained the threat. Elsewhere in the country there was less progress, especially after October 1934, when the TUC issued the 'Black Circular' barring local trades councils from admitting Comunists (and Fascists) and asking unions to enforce similar bans within their own ranks. Even so, Communists were among the most diligent shop stewards and union officials, where they were given the chance. Accustomed to hard work for political ends, and highly committed to the idea of a strongly-organized working class, they 'made a major contribution towards building up the trade unions' (Branson, 1985, p. 185). But this was only part of the reason: growing prosperity was more important in reviving trade unionism after 1933, and the success enjoyed by Communists tended to owe more to their hard work than to their Communism. Indeed, they often fared best when the latter was most hidden form view.

The same applied to their work on behalf of the unemployed. In many ways their 'front' organization, the National Unemployed Workers' Movement (NUWM), can be seen as the party's most successful venture. It certainly filled a vacuum, since many trade unions were too preoccupied to deal with their unemployed members and the Labour Party, fearing a clash with the unions, refused to become involved. It was left to the NUWM, therefore, to advise the unemployed on their rights, represent them at benefit tribunals, and so on. Superficially, the movement's impact was considerable: half a million people were members at some stage during the inter-war period (Harmer, 1988, p. 29). But this 'success' must be qualified. First, while the NUWM was effective in numerous individual cases, it failed to organize the unemployed as a coherent political force, as the party wanted. People joined it for a few weeks while they had a problem, then, satisfied, drifted away again. Secondly, few moved from the NUWM into the CPGB proper. This was even true when the NUWM took a major (though not decisive) role in the UAB crisis of 1935. The movement served, therefore, not to radicalize the workers but, in a sense, to make the existing system more palatable to them: 'only the benefits system gave the NUWM a reason for existence in the eyes of its members; but the con-tinuation of benefits prevented unemployment from becoming the destabilising factor the Communists sought' (Harmer, 1988, pp. 46−7). Similarly, Communist-led hunger marches did little to increase support for the party, or to arouse widespread public sympathy: the 'non-political' Jarrow March of 1936 was far more successful in this respect. The party's efforts, then, made little difference to the country as a whole. Still less did they upset the political structure.

Certainly the Communists played a leading role in tenants' struggles in London and, perhaps even more notably, in the Birmingham rent strike of spring 1939. But these were excep-tional events. There were not many rent strikes in Britain in the 1930s. And, once again, Communists were valued less as Communists than as activists. While party membership in Birmingham increased as a result of the rent strike, only a small fraction of the thousands involved joined the party or had anything to do with it after the immediate crisis was over (Morgan, 1989, p. 285).

It has also been claimed that Communists played a significant role in the struggle against Fascism in Britain. The leadership of the official Labour movement was reluctant to become involved in the politics of street violence. Accordingly, protest was left to Communists − the party leadership, admittedly, having to be prodded into action by an outraged rank-and-file − and ordinary Labourites and trade unionists. Communists were prominent in, for example, the 'Battle of Cable Street' in October 1936 (see below). The Labour leadership, by contrast, was seen as weak by many people who were incapable of understanding that there was more to resisting Fascism than trying to beat up Fascists. Such efforts increased the good will of some Jews and Labour activists towards Communists, but the gains in recruiting terms were not that impressive: few of the 100,000-plus who demonstrated at Cable Street became CPGB members.

Left-wing good will towards the Communists was also increased by their unequivocal support for the Republican cause in the Spanish Civil War. Whereas the Labour response was somewhat muted, not least for fear of losing Catholic support at a time when the Church was backing the Nationalist rebels, the Communists were prominent in organizing men and supplies for Spain. More than half the British volunteers who died fighting for the Republican cause were CPGB members. This added lustre to the party's banner, and undoubtedly encouraged people to join. However, such enthusiasm was being dampened by 1938, as more became known about the tactics of the Spanish Communists in eliminating their supposed allies. Such revelations combined with misgivings about the Soviet show trials to suggest that Communism was not a wholly beneficent creed.

Finally, what about the argument that the Communists played a prominent part in radicalizing sections of opinion? Certainly, there was much interest in the Soviet Union; the Left Book Club (LBC) grew phenomenally following its launch in 1936; and intellectuals did enter the party's ranks. But how significant was the role of the CPGB in all this? The USSR excited the enthusiasm of people across the political spectrum because of the marked contrast between its supposedly planned economy and egalitarian society and what they saw in Britain, particularly in the earlier years of the decade. They were not attracted to the Soviet Union by the CPGB, and they did not join the party because of it. The Left Book Club, set up in 1936 by the publisher Victor Gollancz, was a great success, with almost 60,000 members by 1939. Most of its publications plugged the Communists' popular front line. Yet too much can be made of this. The popular front was not hardline Communism: instead, it offered the more idealistic — or credulous — hope of a more vigorous foreign policy and an end to the National Government at home. The interest it generated did not suggest widespread support for the Marxism-Leninism which still, supposedly, underlay the CPGB's thinking, and which came back to the fore in the autumn of 1939. The vast majority of LBC members had no great sympathy for raw Communism and were to find what they were looking for in the Labour Party as revamped by the Second World War. As for the intellectuals who joined the party in the later 1930s — literary figures like Stephen Spender and W. H. Auden, as well as scientists like J. B. S. Haldane, plus numerous students, doctors and teachers — this was for many, quite literally, a youthful orgasm of rebellion, and in some cases very short-lived. Such members were kept away from the centre of things: they made surprisingly little contribution to the thought of the party, which remained dominated by the Stalinist, Palme Dutt. And, further, it was often among the less immediately influential reaches of the intelligentsia — like teachers — that recruitment was most successful.

In all, then, the Communists were never remotely close to power during the 'Red Decade'. Nor were their policies ever acceptable to more than a fraction of the population. They remained, despite their relatively impressive growth after 1935, very much a minority sect. Where they were able to make some impact, as with the NUWM, or the popular front, it depended to a large extent on how far they were willing to jettison their Communism. Indeed, the 'political irony for the Communist party was the less it spoke of revolution the more sympathy it aroused' (Harmer, 1988, p. 47). At best, their influence was very marginal. While some individuals were won over, the CPGB was, for the vast majority, a political irrelevance.

The same was true, broadly, of the other extreme, despite the fact that the most successful Fascist group ever to exist in Britain, the British Union of Fascists (BUF), was formed in October 1932. It remained in operation until it was closed down by the State in the midst of the deep national crisis of May 1940. The movement and its leader, Sir Oswald Mosley, have aroused considerable controversy, but it is widely agreed that neither came anywhere near to achieving power.

Mussolini's Fascists had taken over in Italy in 1922, and during the remainder of that decade movements on the came far right to rule a number of other European countries. Yet British Fascism in the 1920s was a very sickly child, rarely seen or heard. The British Fascisti (BF), founded in 1923, never had more than a few hundred members at most and by the early 1930s was in terminal decline. It programme comprised little more than hysterical anti-socialism, and its only lasting significance was as a training-ground for people who subsequently moved into the BUF. The Imperial Fascist League (IFL), formed in 1928, was more obviously fascist in orientation. But it came increasingly under the control of Arnold Leese, a retired camel vet of rabidly anti-semitic views, and by the early 1930s its programme was based almost entirely on genocidal rhetoric. Seen alternately as a murderous lunatic and an irritating crank, Leese's difficult personality and off-putting obsessions helped to ensure that the IFL's membership numbered no more than 150 for most of the 1930s.

Such groups could hardly tap the full potential of Fascism in Britain; that task was to be left to Mosley, wealthy scion of gentry family who had been first a Conservative, and then a Labour, MP. In 1929 MacDonald had appointed Mosley to junior office in the second Labour government, with special responsibility for helping to provide employment schemes. Within a year, though, he had resigned in protest against the government's failure to adopt the drastic state action to deal with the problem which he had advocated in the 'Mosley Memorandum'. At the start of 1931 Mosley resigned the Labour whip, and in February the New Party (NP) was launched: five MPs supported him. At first the party seemed to have a bright future: in April, the NP candidate, Allen Young, took 16 per cent of the votes in the Ashton by-election and, arguably, lost Labour the seat. However, this modest performance was to prove the peak of the party's achievement. During the summer of 1931 Mosley's fascist tendencies were becoming so apparent that the party's leading 'left-wingers', Young and John Strachey, resigned; and by the time of the general election that October, Mosley was mainly interested in forming a fighting force, like Mussolini's Blackshirts, rather than playing the parliamentary game. For that reason, and even more because of lack of personnel and prospects, the NP ran only twenty-four candidates at the election; no more than two saved their deposits. No seats were won, the party's newspaper soon folded, and the NP was all but finished.

By the time of the 1931 election, Mosley's programme had moved a long way towards Fascism, and the move was confirmed by his visit to Rome in January 1932, when he met Mussolini. In April he formally disbanded the NP, while keeping the youth movement together as the basis of a Fascist fighting force; and he spent the summer writing *The Greater Britain*, a detailed Fascist programme, and negotiating for a merger with the other Fascist groups. These talks brought only limited success: some BF members joined Mosley, but Leese condemned him as a Jewish-backed opportunist whose 'British Jewnion of Fascists' aimed to neuter the movement with its 'Kosher fascism' (Thurlow, 1987, p. 75). But such mergers were not vital to Mosley's plans, and in October 1932 the BUF was launched.

Superficially, *The Greater Britain* was a programme of considerable force and radicalism, much of it deriving from Mosley's pre-Fascist days. His basic premise was that twentieth-century Britain faced a severe crisis of decline. If action was not taken quickly, she would fall from imperial greatness to impotent decadence as had Spain before her. This apocalyptic vision demanded no half-measures: yet effective action was possible, according to Mosley, given the innate superiority of the Anglo-

51

Saxon races. Nineteenth-century economic and political structures must be replaced. Therefore the BUF proposed the creation of a strictly-disciplined corporate State ruled by a small Cabinet under Mosley. Parliament would remain, but with strictly limited powers; and it would be downgraded, with much of its work passing to twenty-four corporations, each representing all sides of a particular industry and, therefore, every adult in the country. The economic strategy of the corporate State would be to preserve capitalism, though under firm state direction, and to promote self-sufficiency ('autarky') within an imperial trading bloc. The latter would eliminate cheap foreign imports, so enabling British industry to charge high prices and pay high wages. High wages would stimulate demand and thus minimize unemployment.

In other ways, however, the programme was reactionary. There was great reverence for the Monarchy, the Church, and the Empire. Trade union freedoms would be drastically curtailed. Educational policy was even more elitist than that which prevailed at the time. And in stressing traditional gender roles and the family, the BUF was both anti-permissive and 'profoundly anti-feminist' (Lewis, 1987, p. 53). Indeed, like Hitler, Mosley saw the elimination of women from the labour market as being one solution to male unemployment. Unlike Hitler, though, Mosley did not mention the Jews. In fact, at this time his inspiration came from Mussolini – which was hardly surprising given the fact that Hitler had not yet come to power – and this was reflected in the Blackshirt uniform of his followers.

Some aspects, if not the whole, of this programme have attracted praise. But it had many flaws. For example, there was no likelihood of the Dominions, with their own industries growing, agreeing to be part of a hermetically-sealed Empire market, as the National Government was finding at Ottawa even as Mosley was writing his book. Similarly, the restraint on parliament was unlikely to gain widespread support; nor was the suppression of free trade unionism at a time when even many employers were coming to see its positive advantages. Moreover, this programme, if implemented, would have been

52

hostile to the bulk of the population, for 'the corporate state, had it been realised, would in all likelihood have amounted to nothing more than a euphemism concealing a reactionary capitalist dictatorship' (Lewis, 1987, pp. 55–6). The programme, then, lacked coherence except at a superficial level.

However, the BUF attracted not inconsiderable support for a time. Given the fact that economic recovery did not begin until early 1933, this was hardly surprising: the apocalyptic vision convinced many. There was a spectacular growth in membership in late 1933: by February 1934 the BUF had 17,000 members, concentrated largely in London and the north-west of England. Extensive publicity in the Rothermere press then helped to treble membership to around 50,000. Since 1931 there had been a virtual press boycott of Mosley's activities, despite the financial support of some businessmen for the New Party, but now the *Daily Mail*, in particular, lionized the Blackshirts. However, this period of rapid growth came to an abrupt end. Sustained economic recovery made alarmist rhetoric less convincing, and two more spectacular events in June 1934 also hastened the BUF's demise: the brutal treatment of anti-Fascist hecklers by Blackshirt stewards at Mosley's Olympia rally, and Hitler's ruthless suppression of his Nazi critics in the 'Night of the Long Knives'. Both showed the dark side of Fascism at work, and Rothermere, a reactionary Conservative rather than a Fascist, took the opportunity to withdraw his support in July. By October 1935 membership had crashed to 5,000.

The end of the 'Rothermere period' might have made for a 'purer' party, but purity is no asset in politics, and 'the movement all but collapsed as a national force' between then and late 1935 (Thurlow, 1987, p. 103). The only national campaign of 1935 was in opposition to British support for League of Nations sanctions against Italy's invasion of Abyssinia. This was a flop, however, and had been mounted mainly to appease Mussolini, who was supporting the BUF financially (to the tune of £60,000 between 1933 and 1936) (Thurlow, 1987, p. 136). It was this financial support which enabled the movement to maintain its elaborate structure, with 350 employees in 1936, and to mount a series of regional campaigns stressing, for example, the BUF's cotton policy in Lancashire and the shipping policy in Liverpool.

By this time, indeed, such regional campaigns were the staple fare of BUF work. At the 1935 election Mosley, scarred by the humiliation of the New Party in 1931, and realizing the BUF's weakness, put up no candidates but instead campaigned on the less than exhilarating slogan: 'Fascism Next Time'. Attempts to support King Edward VIII against the 'old guard' politicians during the abdication crisis of 1936 were similarly unsuccessful and it was only with the peace campaign, from 1938 onwards, that the movement could be seen once again as a coherent national force.

The most notorious regional campaign was, of course, anti-semitism in the East End of London. Even though Mosley had not mentioned Jews in *The Greater Britain*, anti-semitism had been a feature of his rhetoric since shortly after the BUF's formation. It was played down for a time to placate Rothermere, but in May 1934 Jews were barred from membership of the BUF and, from October, Mosley's speeches became fiercely anti-Jewish. How far Mosley was personally anti-semitic is debatable, but he does seem to have come to the view that Jews enjoyed excessive influence in British life, that they formed the strongest active opposition to the BUF, and that anti-semitism was a useful means of gaining fresh support at a time when his apocalyptic economic analysis seemed unconvincing. In addition, Mosley's frequently-expressed view of Anglo-Saxon superiority suggested that he saw other races as inferior. He also had a number of anti-semitic followers, many of whom were coming to see Hitler rather than Mussolini as their role-model. Thus a mixture of conviction and opportunism led to the highlighting of the Jewish issue.

Such attitudes had a ready audience in London's East End, an area combining great poverty with extensive, and relatively unassimilated, Jewish immigration. From 1936 until the peace campaign of 1938, 'more than half the national membership was concentrated in districts of the East End' (Thurlow, 1987, p. 124). Endemic inter-ethnic violence could now be channelled through the BUF. The boost to support was significant: by the end of 1936, membership had recovered to 15,500, and in the 1937 municipal elections the Fascists came second in a number of East End seats, although never close to victory. However, these modest achievements were made at the expense of considerable violence, both in well-publicized events like the 'Battle of Cable Street' of 4 October 1936 (when a march of 1,900 Fascists was blocked by 100,000 protesters), and in less well-known attacks on Jews and their property, such as the revenge 'pogrom' which followed a week after Cable Street.

All this maximized BUF support in the East End of London: the aftermath of Cable Street, for example, saw 2,000 new recruits being made in the area (Lewis, 1987, p. 111). But quite apart from the moral aspects, the apparent success of the campaign was illusory. First, anti-semitism had little pull outside the area. One-third of the total Jewish population of Britain lived in the East End; in other areas it was less concentrated and tended to be better-assimilated. Furthermore, even in areas of relatively high Jewish population, like Leeds and Manchester, anti-semitism lost, rather than gained, support. Outside these areas the results were even more disastrous: 'the Jewish problem' simply was not a problem, and the BUF's increasing concentration on it merely made it seem irrelevant. It can be no coincidence that by 1937 the movement was collapsing in south Wales, Lancashire, and Birmingham. Secondly, the violence of late 1936 convinced the government that the BUF's activities should be curbed, with the result that the Public Order Act, 1936, banned political uniforms and gave police absolute discretion to ban or re-route marches. The chance to march in uniform had been a major stimulus to recruiting, so it was unsurprising that the BUF's membership, which had been relatively young, 'tough', and drawn from the lower-middle and sections of the working classes, became increasingly bourgeois and conservative during the remainder of the decade. Anti-semitism was a disaster for Fascism in Britain.

Indeed, the movement was in severe difficulties for much of 1937. Membership was low, static, and highly localized.

The flow of Italian money dried up, and Mosley had to increase his own already vast contributions and make cuts in employees (from 350 in 1936 to 50 in 1939) and their salaries. The secession of some members into the stillborn National Socialist League, because they opposed Mosley's autocratic methods and because they wanted still more anti-semitism, seemed to symbolize a deep malaise within the BUF. Even renewed economic recession in late 1937, which should have 'proved' Mosley's apocalyptic arguments, did little to help.

The real boost to membership came with the BUF's opposition to the increasingly likely war with Germany. Such opposition had solid foundations. Many Fascists – including Mosley – had fought in one world war and had no desire to repeat the experience, or to inflict it on their younger compatriots. This was especially so given that Mosley believed that Britain had no fundamental quarrel with Germany. Britain's sphere of interest was the Empire; Germany's was Continental Europe. Britain should no more interfere in Europe than should Germany in the Empire. The First World War, in addition, had seen the spread of Communism, and a further conflict between the non-Communist powers could only further benefit that hated doctrine and the Soviet Union in particular. From 1937 onwards Mosley believed that a commercial radio station, on the lines of Radio Luxembourg, would be an excellent vehicle for BUF propaganda and means of raising money. By 1939 he held shares in various franchises, and Hitler had agreed to build him a transmitter in Germany. A war would (and did) scupper these plans.

The BUF's opposition to the war also raises the question of sympathy with Nazi Germany. Most Fascists were, in fact, intensely patriotic, and few would have considered becoming traitors. This is not to deny that many people, including non-Fascists, admired Hitler and Germany in the 1930s. In the earlier part of the decade a stream of books was published praising the new regime, and as late as 1937 the *Daily Mail*'s foreign correspondent could write of Hitler's 'gay and whimsical' charm and 'good nature' (Ward Price, 1937, pp. 21, 29). But few such books appeared after 1937, and few Fascists contemplated assisting Germany if it came to war, although, characteristically, Leese was to prove an exception.

The peace campaign brought fresh support to the BUF. After two years in the doldrums, membership rose from 16,500 in December 1938 to 22,500 on the outbreak of war nine months later. Yet once again the advance was more apparent than real. In 1938, the BUF was doing little more than replicating the government's popular policy of appeasement. When, in early 1939, the government's line began to change, it followed and was followed by public opinion, with the result that the BUF could only rally the minority of right-wing pacifists. Once again its support was marginalized. The majority of the 10–20,000 who attended a Mosley peace rally at Earl's Court in July 1939 were now older people interested only in Mosley's peace policy, rather than the young enthusiasts for Fascism whom the BUF really wanted. Indeed, many long-time Fascists resigned in protest at the pacifist line being followed.

After the outbreak of war, the BUF continued to campaign for peace. But even in the 'Phoney War' period, when civilian morale was perhaps lower than at any subsequent stage in the conflict, it could make little impact, performing dismally in the by-elections it fought. When the war gathered momentum in May 1940, the State acted swiftly to scratch out the irritant. The BUF was banned and 747 Fascists were interned. This was not because they were seen as a real threat by the government so much as because the new Churchill administration wanted to reassure a public shocked by the Germans' use of fifth columns elsewhere. Smashing British Fascism was a cheap political virility symbol for an embattled government.

Even at its height, British Fascism had never made much impact. Economic recovery and its own desperate excesses in mid-decade had marginalized it still further, and its revival in the last year of peace was again more apparent than real. Mosley, an arrogant, unco-operative, and personally disreputable leader, had a fitting end with internment and, after the war, exile in Ireland and France. Even in the late 1950s, he would feel no compunction about extolling the virtues of Goethe at one moment and at the next telling crowds already inflamed by racial prejudice that West Indians could work for lower wages because they could live off a tin of Kit-E-Kat a day (Skidelsky, 1975, pp. 505, 513). Here was no lost opportunity, no lost leader. British Fascism's pretensions were massive: its performance, dismal and squalid. It never posed a realistic or convincing alternative in the 1930s. Not the least of the achievements of the 'pygmy' politicians of the 1930s − both National and Labour − was that, by shrewd 'hands-off' management and continued appeal to the bulk of the population, they kept the supposed 'giant', Mosley, on the fringe.

CONCLUSION

The politics of the 1930s, for all the controversy they have aroused, were very one-sided. The National Government merely built on the experience of 1929−31 to dominate politics for nearly nine years. During that decade the other parties tried to challenge them, but to little avail. Across Europe, at this time, Communism and Fascism seemed to many to provide the answers sought in the difficult modern world. Yet they had only a very limited appeal in Britain, where the Communist Party and the various Fascist groups, of which the British Union of Fascists was the most significant, enjoyed minimal success, for a number of reasons. There had been no defeat in war, such as to upset the constitution or provide the right with a sense of grievance against the existing system. There had not been extensive demographic dislocation; Mosley's attempts to play on racism, as has been seen, could have little effect, given the limited extent of ethnic problems. The economic slump of 1929−32 was not so deep that it made people despair of a constitutional solution, as was the case in Weimar Germany (see chapter 3). Indeed, at the point of greatest crisis, 1931, the country gave massive support to a government based on a new mix of the old, familiar faces. There was, then, no real opportunity for the Fascists and Communists, although they did not help themselves by their tactical manoeuvres and obvious foreign links (Thorpe, 1988, pp. 1−10). The Liberals, meanwhile, were in such obvious decline that they could not even pretend to have an alternative way forward. This left Labour as the only serious opponent of the National Government, but the legacy of the 1929—31 Labour government, and its own internal divisions, allied to the fact that it remained unable to draw electoral support widely outside sections of the industrial working class and outside its regional heartlands, meant that it never came close to power. In particular, its union-domination meant that it could gain little from the small but growing section of the middle class which was increasingly disenchanted with the rather dull 'expediency politics' of the National Governments.

But those governments were not without achievements: far from it. They could claim that they had allowed prosperity to return during the thirties and generally handled the nation's affairs competently, if with little inspiration. MacDonald, Baldwin, and Chamberlain did not set out to be exciting: excitement meant instability, dictatorship, war, just the things they wanted to avoid. This is not to portray them in too favourable a light, but it is clear that during the decade they gave enough people — and sizeable sections of the working class supported them at the polls — what they wanted, or, at least, less of what they did not want than the other parties could offer. Even in 1940, when Chamberlain fell, it was due largely to a revolt within the Conservative Party: and the majority of MPs were behind him. The politics of the 1930s were the politics of National hegemony, supported by the bulk of the population, to whom they certainly seemed more attractive than their opponents.

3

The Economy

The hegemony of the National Government cannot be fully understood solely by reference to politics, however. In particular, analysis of the workings of the British economy in the 1930s adds force to the arguments of the previous chapter. Yet, once again, this has been an area of considerable debate. So what were the trends of depression and prosperity during the decade? How far was the economy being restructured away from the nineteenth-century pattern towards a 'modern' mode? Why did government follow the policy it did, and were viable alternatives available?

CYCLICAL TRENDS

The First World War and its aftermath had produced massive problems for the British economy; many of them were to persist throughout the inter-war period. Firstly, Britain had been forced to abandon the gold standard, by which the value of sterling was fixed. Yet the gold standard was seen, during the 1920s, as the basis of a stable currency, and even under the 1918–22 Lloyd George Coalition moves had been afoot to facilitate a return to it by cutting expenditure and taxation and attempting to reduce inflation. When it was restored, in 1925, it almost certainly overpriced British exports. But the British economy, and especially the old staple industries – coal, iron and steel, cotton, and shipbuilding – relied heavily on export markets. The effects were, therefore, severe. This was especially so since the war had forced these industries to produce mainly for (temporary) wartime needs at home: foreign markets were lost as countries found alternative suppliers or built up those industries themselves. The post-war speculative boom worsened matters as investors poured money into the temporarily prosperous staple industries. Over-capacity led, from the later twenties, to attempts to 'rationalize' them by forcing amalgamations and closing down excess capacity; the main short-term effect was to increase unemployment. And while unemployment weakened the workers' position generally, wages, which had been raised during the post-war boom, were difficult to cut, at a time when this would have been the orthodox means of reducing export prices. Finally, the war had also increased the national debt massively: by the later 1920s, servicing the war debt was costing around 40 per cent of all central government expenditure (Aldcroft, 1986, p. 24). The advances of newer industries, like motor-car maunfacture, helped to boost the economy, but the staples were still so significant a sector that, if they could not prosper, then the economy as a whole could enjoy only partial prosperity at best.

The economy had taken some time to settle even into that. The manic boom had been followed by recession in 1920–1, with the economy moving from full employment to 22 per cent unemployment (2.4 million) in the year to May 1921 in what has been described as 'one of the worst recessions in history' (Aldcroft, 1986, p. 6). While the next few years saw improvement, it should be noted that Britain's 'boom' of the 1920s was feeble compared with those in the United States and Germany; unemployment was not to fall below a million again until 1940. The economy never really got going in the inter-war years.

The response of 1920s governments was distinctly conservative. This was symbolized by the emphasis placed on the return to gold – every effort should be made to restore the conditions under which, it was believed, pre-war industry had prospered. Government should balance the budget, keep tax burdens off

61

industry as far as possible, and wait for better times to come. This was clearly the line of the Conservative administration of 1924−9, and became encapsulated in its slogan at the 1929 election: 'Safety First'. But in reality the policy of Labour, under MacDonald and Snowden, was little different in the short term, since both believed in the inevitable rise of a socialist society from the success of capitalism. At the 1929 election Labour's commitment to public-works schemes to cure unemployment was mainly rhetorical. Lloyd George had foisted a more radical policy on to the Liberal party, but there is now little support for the view that he could substantially have increased employment by deficit-financed public works while maintaining the three fundamentals − parliamentary democracy, free trade, and the gold standard − in which Liberals still believed. In any case, his party, as seen above, had no hope of victory.

The debates at the 1929 election had assumed a continuation of the limited boom of the later 1920s. But, in fact, the indicators were already pointing towards recession, with export orders falling off dramatically towards the end of 1928; and when this was followed, a year later, by a slump throughout most of the Western world, there was to be no escape for Britain, dependent as she was on world markets. In particular, the collapse of the American economy, and the increase in American tariffs to record high levels, not only cut British exports to that country, but also reduced the purchasing power of Britain's other customers, since American loans and imports were also curtailed.

Throughout 1930 the balance of trade worsened and unempolyment rose inexorably: among workers covered by unemployment insurance it nearly doubled. During the tenure of the second Labour government (June 1929 to August 1931) it increased from 1.1 to 2.8 million. Many more were on short time, or unemployed but not on the register. The sheer magnitude of the increase must be stressed, for it jolted people out of their belief that pre-war 'normalcy' could ever be restored. It helped to pave the way for the more innovatory policies of the 1930s. The increase in unemployment also had another major impact. The Lloyd George Coalition had extended unemployment insurance to virtually all industrial workers, and had also introduced a system whereby workers who had exhausted their entitlement to insurance benefit could claim special payments (variously called transitional or uncovenanted benefit) to prevent them from having to resort to the unpopular and demeaning Poor Law. Hence, as unemployment rose, government expenditure also rose dramatically. To finance this, it was necessary to increase taxes and borrowing; business confidence fell accordingly. By mid−1931 the unemployment insurance fund was clearly bankrupt, and Exchequer support for it was threatening seriously to unbalance the national budget.

At the same time, the trade balance took a turn for the worse. Britain's demand for imports − like essential food supplies − was less elastic than other countries' demand for its exports. To further aggravate matters, 'invisible' exports like shipping were also collapsing as a result of the reduced volume of trade. The result was that a £104 million trade surplus in 1928 became a £114 million deficit in 1931 (Aldcroft, 1986, p. 47).

Three of the first six months of 1931 saw slight falls in unemployment, but any signs of recovery were over shadowed by the financial crisis which forced the Labour government from office in August and compelled the National Government to abandon the gold standard a month later. Until the end of the year the jobless total fell steadily and it appeared that prosperity might be returning. The departure from gold devalued the pound and so reduced export prices; business confidence was increased by the installation of a perceivedly more competent and sympathetic government with a policy of protective tariffs; and the firm resolve of the government to balance the budget reassured opinion both at home and abroad. But while this recovery helped the government to win a sweeping victory at that October's general election, it was merely temporary: unemployment began to rise again early in 1932, and peaked that August at 23 per cent of the insured workforce: in all, 3,750,000 workers were probably out of work (Pollard, 1983, p. 155). Then, however, the economy did begin to revive.

A number of points should be noted about 1929–32. First, the slump in Britain was neither especially severe nor prolonged when compared to those experienced by Germany and the United States. Secondly, again in contrast to those countries, it was not preceded by a spectacular boom in the 1920s. The shock, therefore, was not as great. Thirdly, while all sectors of the economy experienced adverse effects, it was in the old staple industries that the effects were worst: steel production, for example, fell from 9.6 million tons in 1929 to 5.2 in 1931, recovering somewhat to 7.0 million in 1933, whereas motor-vehicle production, overall, increased by 20 per cent between 1929 and 1933 (Mitchell and Deane, 1962, p. 137; Allen, 1970, p. 154).

Between the third quarter of 1932 and the end of 1933 things improved vigorously, with insured unemployment falling to 17.5 per cent. During 1934 recovery continued, but at a slacker pace, and in 1935 greater momentum was resumed. By late 1935, although unemployment remained high, there were signs of a booming economy such as shortages of skilled labour in key areas. Recovery continued until the third quarter of 1937, by which time insured unemployment had fallen to around 9 per cent (1.4 million) — still seen as too high, but increasingly a regional phenomenon, concentrated in areas like south Wales and north-eastern England which were dependent on export trades. Even Keynes, the leading advocate of increased government spending to reduce unemployment (see below), was warning in 1937 of the dangers of inflation unless there was budgetary caution, given the boom conditions that were being enjoyed by much of the country (Peden, 1980, p. 1).

The reasons for Britain's economic recovery in the mid-1930s have been much debated. A number of factors were at work. There was a boom in construction, helped by the low interest rates maintained by the National Government from 1932, and meeting a demand for housing created by a demographic shift towards smaller families which had not been satisfied by the limited construction programme of the 1920s. This had a number of beneficial effects. Building was labour-intensive and so many new jobs were created; activity was nationwide and so stimulated the economy as a whole; and it increased demand in many other industries, not only those concerned with building materials but also those producing the consumer durables necessary to furnish a home. Few historians would, indeed, dispute the key role of the building boom in promoting and prolonging recovery of the economy.

The second agent of recovery was the development of 'new' industries and service industries, although their exact role remains a talking point and will be discussed in the next section. Here it is sufficient to note that they were certainly expanding. Motor-vehicle production rose from 306,000 in 1932 to 586,000 in 1937; radio production, from 506,000 in 1930 to 1,918,000 in 1937. Output of man-made fibres more than doubled between 1929 and 1937 (Allen, 1970, pp. 177, 203, 301). Employment in service industries, meanwhile, increased by 1.2 million between 1931 and 1939.

There can be no doubt, also, that recovery was boosted by a modest improvement, certainly in 1934–5, in the staple industries, to which Britain's economy was still heavily committed. This was due partly to a revival of exports, although it was patchy – steel fared better than coal, for example – and even in 1937 the staples' export volume was 20 per cent below the medicre figure for 1929 (Mitchell and Deane, 1962, p. 306). They were helped by the construction boom, which stimulated demand in some areas. While it would not do to exaggerate the point, recovery of the staple indutries was a contributory factor to the overall economic improvement evident by 1937.

The general easing of world economic circumstances after 1933 also helped Britain. Exports to the USA, for example, increased from £15.1 million in 1932 to £31.4 million five years later; and the recovery of the American economy also improved the position of Britain's other overseas customers, enabling them to buy more British exports.

The role of government policy in promoting recovery will be discussed below, and it is sufficient to say here that the National administration's policies assisted matters in a number of ways; in any case, the mere existence of an apparently competent

65

government committed fully to the maintenance of capitalism steadied nerves and increased confidence after the perceived chaos of two years of Labour rule.

By mid-1937, then, the British economy was booming, with shortages of skilled labour, inflationary pressures, and a significant increase in imports. Almost one worker in every ten was still out of work, but most of that unemployment was due to structural factors. From the perspective of 1937, the average annual growth rate since 1924 was 2.2 per cent, by no means unimpressive in British terms, comparing as it did with an identical figure for 1856–73 and 2.8 per cent for 1951–73 (Middleton, 1985, p. 21).

In the third quarter of 1937, however, the boom broke. There followed a sharper, though less general, cyclical downturn than that of 1929–30. To a certain extent it was an imported recession, following the break in American recovery, but the satiation of domestic demand for many products also played its part. So did deflationary monetary policies from a government nervous that the economy was overheating. Overall, unemployment increased from 10.1 per cent in September 1937 to 13.8 per cent in June 1938, with the export and durable manufacturing industries bearing the brunt (Capie and Collins, 1980, p. 48). Unemployment in steel rose from 11.4 per cent in 1937 to 19.5 per cent in 1938; in cotton textiles, from 10.9 to 23.9 per cent; in woollen textiles, from 8.8 to 21.3 per cent. Even in a 'new' industry like motors and aircraft it rose from 5.0 to 7.2 per cent. (Mitchell and Deane, 1962, p. 67).

This suggested that the advances of the 1930s were not invulnerable to cyclical pressures, and Capie and Collins have argued that only government action (in the form of deficit-financed rearmament to meet the German threat) prevented some sectors of the economy 'falling very far' (1980, p. 57). Without this expenditure, unemployment might have reached, not 1.8 million, but 3 million in 1938; with it, the recession was over by September of that year, although unemployment was to remain above a million until 1940 (Thomas, 1983, p. 571). This in turn casts at least some doubt on the view that

66

the economy was successfully restructuring itself around a 'development block' of dynamic new industries.

STRUCTURAL CHANGE

The fact that unemployment remained at almost 10 per cent at the height of the boom in 1937 suggests that analysis of cyclical trends alone tells only part of the story of the performance of the British economy in the 1930s. Structural features must also be taken into account. The country entered the decade over-committed to old staple industries — textiles, iron and steel, coal, mechanical engineering, and shipbuilding — which were heavily reliant on exports and yet which could no longer sell anything approaching their full capacity of production. Agriculture fared better, while the 'new' industries — like motor manufacturing, electrical engineering, man-made fibres, chemicals — made massive strides forward. But what were the effects on employment? And how far was the 1930s economy being restructured out of a 'late Victorian' mode?

There can be no disputing the fact that the staple industries were a significant drag on the economy throughout the 1930s. The problem was basically two-fold: there was a fall in demand for their products, and even where there was demand, Britain often could not compete with other producers on cost or quality grounds. This left the British staples in a difficult position. There were attempts, some of them government-sponsored, to 'rationalize' these industries by eliminating surplus capacity, but such schemes had only limited success, and in any case had few positive short-term effects on employment. Jarrow, where Palmer's shipyard was dismantled in mid-decade as part of a national drive to reduce capacity, lives on in the popular memory as 'the town that was murdered' rather than as a case of rationalization producing beneficial effects. The formation of price-fixing cartels, most notably in steel, was another solution, but again only a very partial one. Gradually the proportion of resources devoted to the staple industries did

67

decline (with significant disinvestment during the recovery of 1932–37), but it was a painful process and since, even in 1937, they still accounted for more than a quarter of total net output, they remained a problem which could not be ignored.

Agriculture, however, improved its performance for a number of reasons. The protection given to farmers in most other countries suggested that Britain could not stand alone for free trade. Governments became convinced that massive food imports were destabilizing the fragile balance of trade. The Conservative Party, which dominated government from 1931 onwards, had been made more receptive to farmers' demands by the widespread defection of the agricultural vote to the Liberals in 1929. And finally, as war came to look more and more likely later in the decade, it seemed prudent to rely less on imports. These considerations led to extensive government assistance to agriculture. Protection was imposed in 1931–32. Direct subsidies were provided to the producers of wheat and sugar beet. And the government also built on the Agricultural Marketing Act of 1931, which allowed producers of any commodity to set up marketing boards. Even so, while all this shored up agriculture, it did not set off a great boom. Indeed, its rather ambiguous results probably confirmed the suspicions of many observers about government assistance to other industries.

But it was the new industries which expanded most impressively as they reduced their costs and as demand grew. In these industries, 1929 levels of production had been 'almost regained by 1933' (Johnman, 1986, p. 233). The new industries had many advantages. They produced mainly for the home market, which was less subject to serious fluctuations than the export trade. They had newer equipment, and so could compete on more equal cost terms with other countries. And, generally speaking, they had fewer labour relations problems because trade union and management practices were less entrenched.

But how impressive was their performance? The notion that they constituted a 'development bloc', leading the nation to new, higher levels of growth, has come in for considerable criticism, and no longer seems wholly tenable. Structural change advanced slowly, and the export trades continued to have a central place. Even so, the growth of the new industries cannot be denied, both in absolute terms and in their share of total output, as seen in table 3.1.

TABLE 3.1   *Contribution of 'new' and 'old' industries to total net output (Value)* (%)

	'New'	'Old'
1924	14.1	37.0
1930	15.9	29.6
1935	21.0	27.8

Source: S. Pollard: *The Development of the British Economy 1914–1980* (1983), p. 54

The economy was taking on a new structure, but unspectacularly. In the light of these figures it would be rash to argue that the new industries led Britain out of recession after 1932. Instead the country saw a general recovery, in which the building boom played a leading part.

The shift which took place was therefore limited in scope; and the staples were not being quietly replaced. Far from it. The new industries tended to be based in the south-east and the Midlands, nearer their markets and away from areas noted for trade union traditions. This meant prosperity, and sometimes feverish boom conditions, in those areas; but it also meant that there was no direct replacement of 'old' by 'new' in areas like south Wales and, consequently, there were huge regional discrepancies. The unemployment problem changed from one of very high numbers of short- to medium-term jobless over most of the country, to one of lower numbers unemployed for longer stretches in certain areas (see table 3.2). Of those out of work for over a year, 38 per cent of the whole sample had been unemployed for more than five years, but the figure was 44 per cent in the Rhondda, 51 per cent in Blackburn, and 71 per cent in Crook (Pilgrim Trust, 1938, p. 422). Structural unemployment had replaced cyclical as the main problem, and this in itself posed problems to policymakers, for it was soon clear that to eliminate the regional

TABLE 3.2 *Long-term unemployment in six towns (November 1936)*

	% unemployed	% unemployed for a year or more
Deptford (London)	6.7	0.4
Leicester	7.4	0.8
Liverpool	25.7	5.9
Blackburn	29.5	11.2
Crook (Co. Durham)	33.6	18.8
Rhondda (S. Wales)	44.5	28.1

Source: Pilgrim Trust: *Men Without Work* (1938), p. 15

extremes of poverty and prosperity would take more than simply stimulating the centre, as Keynes himself had recognized by 1937. Thus, if the economy was being restructured in the 1930s, it was a process which had a long way to go before it could bring anything approaching full employment to Britain as a whole. And it was widely held that many of the long-term unemployed might never work again. The fact that they did was due to the outbreak of war in 1939 and its continuation for six years.

GOVERNMENT ECONOMIC POLICY: CAUSES AND EFFECTS

The National Governments have often been seen as doing little to help in the face of these difficulties. For traditionalists, there was a battle between the government and 'orthodoxy' on the one hand, and 'Keynesianism', which took its name from the economist John Maynard Keynes (1883–1946), whose *General Theory* was published in 1936, on the other. Keynes was firmly committed to capitalism, but he believed that the power of the State could be used to maximize prosperity and employment. For example, during a recession, the government should borrow money and spend it on measures, like road-building, which would provide employment. The deficit could then be paid back out of future prosperity. Traditionally, this approach has been seen as battling against the prevailing 'Treasury view' which held that government could not, and should not try to, stimulate employment by 'artificial' means, but should work instead to create conditions in which private enterprise could flourish — for example, by balancing the national budget and creating business 'confidence'. Historians writing in the post-war decades believed that the 'full employment' of those years was largely due to 'Keynesian' policies: hence, by refusing to adopt them, 1930s governments had been almost criminally negligent, refusing to listen to sensible advice and, instead, sitting on their hands, governed by ignorance, timidity, or malice, or a combination of all three. But this is too simplistic. In fact, there were innovations in government economic policy during the thirties, and there were also sound reasons for not being more interventionist.

The National Governments were, of course, firmly committed to private enterprise. Of the three Prime Ministers, Baldwin and Chamberlain were businessmen, while MacDonald's socialism had always been based on the belief that the reforms which would lead to the millennium could only be paid for by the success of capitalist enterprise. They believed that high taxation and government borrowing would reduce the competitive potential of British industry, sap initiative and lead the country into a mire of decline from which no one, least of all the working class, would profit. Thus the first duty of government was to maintain business confidence, especially through keeping a tight rein on government expenditure and balancing the budget. However, these governments were not averse to more imaginative policies, always providing that they conformed with the established nostra of what it was proper for a government to do, and a number of these stand out in particular: protectionism, low interest rates, a managed exchange rate, and the development of regional policy to help the most depressed areas.

A balanced budget was seen to be the key to all else. The Labour Chancellor between 1929 and 1931, Snowden, fought hard to maintain a balance. However, faced with falling revenues due to the slump, and with colleagues reluctant, for political and humanitarian reasons, to restrain expenditure, he had a difficult time. By the start of 1931 a heavy budget deficit was widely expected, and business interests and both Conservatives and Liberals were clamouring for 'economy measures'. The prediction by the May Committee of a £120 million deficit that July made these imperative. The Labour Cabinet could not agree on cuts large enough to satisfy anyone except themselves, but the National Government which succeeded it imposed cuts of 10 per cent in benefits and most public servants' salaries. Taxes were increased and annual budgets showed a small surplus until the costs of rearmament and a fall in revenues following the recession produced a small deficit for 1937, and a much larger one the following year. Budgetary policy remained cautious; the 1931 cuts were not restored until 1934, and taxes were cut only slowly, and began to rise again in 1936.

The effects of budgetary policy have aroused much debate. In particular, Middleton has argued that the bare budget balance did not reflect its true impact (1985). He points out that, taking into account local government expenditure, public spending was severely tightened until 1933–34; argues that the 'crisis' measures were maintained too long after the onset of recovery, so hindering the latter process; and concludes that it was 'most fortunate' that a relaxation of fiscal orthodoxy (that is, borrowing for rearmament) followed the 1937 recession. Yet, as he himself admits, the government had little room for manoeuvre here. Above all, it had to maintain confidence, and in the 1930s that could only be done by ensuring that the budget balanced in the conventional way. Thus while budgetary policy might have had adverse effects, they were not as great as those which might have resulted from a 'less orthodox' policy.

But the National Governments were far from being blindly conservative. Between 1929 and 1931 there had been a considerable shift of public and business opinion away from free trade (in 1930 the Federation of British Industries stated that 96 per cent of its members wanted tariffs), a process reflected in the Conservative Party's adoption of a fully protectionist programme in October 1930. Most Tories had worried that participation in a National Government might lead to the dilution of this policy; and, indeed, at the 1931 election the government called only for a free hand to take whatever measures it saw fit to rectify the trade imbalance. However, most Conservative candidates and spokesmen declared unequivocally for protection, and there could be little, if any, doubt that it would be introduced (Thorpe, 1991, pp. 219–54). Temporary duties were imposed immediately, and in 1932 the Import Duties Act and the agreement of limited imperial preference with the Dominions restored Britain to protectionism. The position at the end of that year was that about a quarter of imports were duty-free, half paid a tariff of between 10 and 20 per cent, 8 per cent paid over 20 per cent and the rest were covered by previous measures of protection (Pollard, 1983, p. 121).

What were the results? Chamberlain hoped it would be a turning-point in British history, but Capie has argued that '[in] terms of what Chamberlain was looking for, . . . the tariff can hardly be considered a success', and that its 'role in stimulating the manufacturing sector in the 1930s must have been small' (1983, pp. 139–40). However, this is probably too harsh a view. While tariffs did not usher in a new period of astounding prosperity, they did stop the tide of dumping and prevented matters from getting worse. Secondly, the business community had been clamouring for protection: the satisfaction of their demands therefore boosted confidence. And, thirdly, while no Empire trading bloc emerged as a result of imperial preference, there was a significant shift of trade towards the Empire. By 1937, 37.3 per cent of Britain's imports came from the Empire, and 39.7 per cent of its exports went to it, as opposed to 24.5 per cent of imports and 32.6 per cent of exports in 1931 (Pollard, 1983, p. 123). Overall, then, protection had a beneficial effect, though it was by no means as great as many Conservatives had hoped.

It seems more certain that the government's establishment and preservation of low interest rates for most of the decade helped the economy. During the later 1920s the bank rate had crept up, rising to 4½ per cent in July 1931 and 6 per cent after the departure from gold that September. However, as monetary pressures eased, it was cut, until in June 1932 it stood at 2 per cent, where it remained for seven years. In the 1920s, high interest rates had hindered the domestic economy; now, cheap money provided a valuable stimulus, most notably in facilitating the housing boom which bore considerable responsibility for lifting Britain out of the slump. This was not the sole, nor even the main, aim of the Treasury or the Bank of England; at least as important was the desire to reduce the cost of servicing the national debt, and to discourage inflows of speculative money, the withdrawal of which on the slightest pretext might have led − or so it was believed − to another financial crisis on the lines of 1931. Even so, cheap money was a major contribution by government to prosperity in the 1930s.

Another innovation was the exchange equalization account established in April 1932. This was a second-best option for a government formed to preserve the gold standard; but once forced off gold, the alternative was soon accepted. Whatever its other failings, the government never seriously reconsidered a return to gold. The exchange equalization account received Treasury money which it used to buy and sell sterling so as to negate forces destabilizing the exchange rate. It was a compromise between the shackles of gold and the potential anarchy of a floating pound, and insofar as it kept the value of sterling reasonably steady and made export prices lower than they had been, it helped exporters and business confidence generally.

The fourth innovation was the introduction of regional policy, as a measure to combat the structural unemployment noted above. By 1934, with recovery progressing strongly in most of Britain but assuredly not in the depressed areas reliant on the old staple industries, it could no longer be argued convincingly that a cyclical upturn in the economy would solve the unemployment problems of the country as a whole. Thus the Special Areas Act, 1934, appointed one commissioner for central Scotland (excluding Glasgow) and one for north-eastern England, west Cumberland, and south Wales. The two commissioners had a budget with which to promote enterprise in these areas. But while this was step in the right direction, it would be rash to make great claims for it. Special schemes to help distressed areas were not unprecedented: the 1920s had seen various schemes to assist the transfer of 'surplus labour' from depressed to prosperous areas. These had hardly been successful, though, and had withered away during the general depression of 1929–32. What was new in the 1930s was the recognition of the need to deal, in however limited a way, with the problems of the depressed areas *per se* rather than trying to obviate them through transference. Secondly, the way in which the policy came about suggested no overnight conversion to regionalism on the part of government. Chamberlain, in particular, was contemptuous of the intellectual arguments for regional policy, but accepted it as politically necessary, especially after a series of articles in the normally friendly *Times* in March 1934 had highlighted the problems of the depressed areas. Political considerations loomed large: the government hoped to retain some of the seats won unexpectedly in these areas in 1931 and, more realistically, to reassure its supporters in other parts of the country that something was being done about the situation. Thirdly, many badly-affected areas, like Northern Ireland and Lancashire, were not included in the scheme. Fourthly, the emphasis of the legislation remained very much on enabling private enterprise to flourish: the powers of the two commissioners were strictly circumscribed, and they could not spend any of their meagre budgets (£1 million a year each) on the direct provision of employment, or on direct subsidies to firms. Indeed, their powers were so limited that the commissioner for England and Wales resigned in frustration in 1936. Although legislation in 1936 and 1937 augmented the commissioners' powers and aimed to encourage the introduction of new industries in the depressed areas, this had little effect: new industries still had good reasons for, and nothing to prevent them from, establishing themselves in the more prosperous south and Midlands. However, some trading estates were set up in areas of high unemployment, and became one of the few tangible benefits of 1930s regional policy. It was rearmament and war, of course, that eventually revived these areas by reviving the staple industries.

This policy of limited involvement in the economy had a

vital concomitant: a reasonably flexible pattern of state benefits for the unemployed and their dependents. The drastic increase in unemployment between 1929 and 1931 had effectively bankrupted the unemployment insurance fund, with a resultant rise in state expenditure, and benefits had risen in real terms due to falling prices. It was over the necessity, or otherwise, of cutting benefits that the Labour government fell in 1931. The National Government immediately cut benefits and introduced means-testing; later, in 1935, it reorganized the whole system. A number of factors influenced benefits policy in the 1930s. First was the conviction that state expenditure should be kept within bounds. The fear of many members of all parties, and of officials, during the 1929–31 Labour government had been that financial control had been effectively abandoned. The National Government, as noted above, soon signalled its reimposition. In addition, it held the view that benefits should preserve the old principle of 'less eligibility' – they should always be lower than wages, so as not to push up wage levels or discourage people from working. It was hoped also that the insurance principle would be maintained as far as possible. However, the pressure was not only downward. Governments believed that the system had a key role to play in maintaining social peace, a subject on which Conservative politicians in particular were rather nervous throughout the inter-war period. This meant that the 'respectable' unemployed should be preserved from the stigma of the Poor Law, and that benefit levels should not be so low as to make some semblance of normal life impossible. Finally, the National Governments were keen to keep benefit issues out of party politics: they had become a political football in 1931 and, while everything had turned out well then, a repeat performance might not have the same 'happy' ending. After all, the potential venality of a fledgling democracy – universal adult suffrage had only been conceded in 1928 – was a major element in the thinking of many older Conservatives, including Baldwin. Given the collapse of parlimentary government across much of Europe, such concerns were understandable, if wrong-headed.

These hopes and fears came together in the Unemployment

Act, 1934, and its aftermath, the UAB crisis of early 1935 (see chapter 2). The most significant aspect of that crisis in this context is that it showed that the government recognized the centrality of payments to the unemployed in its overall economic strategy, and that it was pragmatic enough to bend when necessary in order to maintain the essentials of that strategy intact. (Ultimately, and after the 1935 election, standardization of benefits was pushed through.) Of course, this involved a compromise: benefits probably kept wages, and so production costs, somewhat higher than they would otherwise have been, and produced a very small amount of 'voluntary' unemployment. But for the government, benefit policy was a success insofar as it reduced the demands for a more interventionist economic strategy.

Thus government in the 1930s decided on an innovative ring-holding operation rather than a more directly interventionist policy. But could more have been done to reduce unemployment? In the halcyon days of full employment and low inflation during and after the Second World War, the generally-held view was that Keynesian methods of demand management would have produced full employment in Britain in the 1930s. Government, in spending money on public works, would not only have provided work directly, but also, through the stimulation of extra demand, have boosted the economy as a whole. If it did not have the money, it should have borrowed it, since the resultant economic activity would soon have produced a bonanza in tax revenue. It was a central tenet of the 'Devil's Decade' view that a solution existed but that it was never tried by 1930s governments for a variety of unwholesome reasons. Although no historian today would go as far as this, some can still be found arguing that a Keynesian alternative would have worked, at least to some extent (Garside & Hatton, 1985). The balance of the historiography, however, has swung very much in the opposite direction since the early 1970s, when Keynesian methods began to 'fail' in Britain. In the 1950s and early 1960s, it had seemed that Keynesianism was the key to success; from the later perspective, doubt could be poured on this view as it became clear that economic success then had been helped by other factors, such as cheap oil and the needs of post-war reconstruction. In addition, the opening of archives has given a fuller picture of economic policy-making, and it is now reasonable to argue that government in the 1930s was wise to follow the policies that it did.

The line taken both by the Labour government and its National successors, to reiterate, was that private enterprise had to pull Britain out of the recession and that state 'interference' could only hinder that process. For all their innovations in exchange rate management and the like, the philosophy of governments until the Second World War changed little from the classic exposition of the 'Treasury view' put forward by Churchill, as Chancellor of the Exchequer, in 1929: that 'very little additional employment and no permanent employment [could] in fact and as a general rule be created by State borrowing and State expenditure' (Peden, 1983, p. 281). Some historians have purported to see a process of conversion to Keynesianism at work within the Treasury in the late 1930s, but the evidence is highly debatable: indeed, others are now questioning whether there was even a 'Keynesian revolution' in the 1940s (Booth, 1989). Rearmament, though deficit-financed, stemmed from needs of national security rather than the intellectual conversion of Treasury mandarins; indeed, most National politicians and civil servants were concerned that it might set a precedent for future assaults on budgetary orthodoxy and the primacy of private enterprise within the economy.

A number of factors help to explain the government's reluctance to take a more interventionist line. The generally-felt need to maintain confidence perhaps acted as the major constraint. It has been suggested that the 'Treasury view' (by encouraging business to believe that only a balanced budget could be 'sound') was self-fulfilling, but this is too simplistic an explanation. The 'Treasury view' was not something cooked up by a few civil servants, a kind of evil brew concocted by bankers like Montagu Norman and civil servants like Warren Fisher as they ate the babies of the working class in the dungeons of Whitehall. It was the product of a century or more of thinking about 'sound finance'. As such, it affected politicians, financiers and businessmen in the same way. Confidence had been wanting in 1929–31, especially when large budget deficits had looked likely. Depression had been the result. Government was always afraid, during the 1930s, that another, worse, depression was on the way: to keep it at bay the State must ensure that its financial rectitude was beyond reproach. As even Garside admits, most contemporary politicians, financiers, and industrialists viewed an unbalanced budget as 'a fearful prospect' (1985, p. 551). For in Europe at the time there were worse things happening than unemployment, even for the unemployed: threats to democracy, threats to peace, and threats to Britain's world position (with all the implications they could have for domestic living standards). It was seen as too much of a gamble to start experimenting with unemployment if this was likely to destroy confidence, destabilize the economy, and jeopardize the established political system and the bases of Britain's world power. The main Treasury complaint against Keynes was that he seemed to disregard the need to maintain confidence (Middleton, 1982, p. 55). Only the Second World War and its aftermath changed general perceptions sufficiently to allow 'Keynesian' policies to be contemplated with something approaching equanimity.

Confidence was not the only constraining factor, however. The trade balance was a great worry, being 'decidedly unhealthy' throughout the decade (Drummond, 1981, p. 300). Protection helped, but not sufficiently to provide a margin adequate to finance a substantial increase in imports. Yet an active employment policy meant reflation of the economy, and this would be likely to suck in imports and so result in a serious trade deficit. Further protective measures might have prevented this, but they were likely to offend many people, including the Conservatives' allies in the National Government. Similarly, increased exports would have righted the balance, but short of direct subsidies – which no one was advocating – it was difficult to see how this could be achieved in the short term. The need to maintain the trade balance in difficult circumstances, then, provided a further argument against government intervention.

79

The size of the national debt, which had risen from £620 million in 1914 to £7,810 million in 1920 as a result of borrowing for the war effort, also posed serious problems (Mitchell and Deane, 1962, p. 403). In the later 1920s, interest payments on it amounted to around a third of government expenditure, and in 1932, the peak year, servicing the national debt cost 8.2 per cent of national income (Tomlinson, 1978, p. 72). A major conversion of the debt to a lower rate of interest then eased matters, but it continued to inhibit policy-makers for two reasons. Servicing the debt still cost a great deal of money: in 1936, for example, over a quarter of gross state expenditure went in this way. Secondly, these payments proved such a millstone that politicians and civil servants were reluctant to burden themselves and future generations with further loans to finance public works, especially when they believed that such works would have, at best, limited and transitory benefits. In any case, the prevailing interest rate of 2 per cent was unlikely to attract large amounts of money to a loan issue, so the bank rate might have to be raised, destroying the cheap money policy which had so aided recovery since 1932.

Indeed, the prospect of mortgaging the future to finance jobs in the short term revived, among civil servants and most National politicians, fears which had been generated by Lloyd George in 1929 and by Labour two years later – that politicians would seek to buy votes by promising, irresponsibly, an ever-increasing spiral of public expenditure, and of 'creating a series of vested interests which would endanger long-run economic and political stability' (Middleton, 1982, p. 64). Keynes rejected this view, arguing that good sense would prevail, but most Treasury men saw this as mere assertion, and unconvincing at that (Peden, 1983, p. 283). If 'right-minded' governments adopted such practices, then there would be no hope of re-straining a future Labour administration from profligate expen-diture. While the experience of the 'sound' financial management of Labour governments since the Second World War enables us to doubt this, such hindsight was unavailable in the 1930s; at the 1931 election, in particular, the Labour Party had promised considerable increases in expenditure with little, if any, real idea of the sources of the extra revenue it would require (Thorpe, 1991, pp. 219–54).

Administrative constraints were another obstacle to intervention. The most likely method of implementing public works was through the local authorities, which undertook most direct public capital investment at the time. Yet here lay the problem. Although central grants were becoming more important, local authorities still had considerable autonomy and could not be treated simply as an arm of central government. Public works would have required either an open-handed system of grants from centre to locality, the expenditure of which would have been very difficult to control; or else a revolution in central – local relations on a scale that few could have contemplated with equanimity. A central planning agency with almost dictatorial powers would also have been needed, as the more coherent plans for public works, such as those of Mosley, recognized (Middleton, 1982, 66–9). To fight the constitutional battles that would inevitably have arisen would have required an immense expenditure of effort for questionable gains. In addition, plans for roads and other such schemes took time to prepare, and it would not have been easy to co-ordinate the start of works with a cyclical downturn. It is not surprising, then, that when it wanted to disparage public works as a way of boosting the economy, the Treasury focused on the practical and administrative difficulties involved. They were, to all intents and purposes, 'insuperable' (Middleton, 1985, p. 180).

Given these constraints, it is doubtful whether any alternative policy could have been more successful in reducing unemployment. The fact remained that Britain in the 1930s faced not one unemployment problem, but two: cyclical unemployment, which could, theoretically at least, be alleviated by central 'demand management'; and structural unemployment, for which the solutions were either a more active regional policy or a reduction in costs to make British exports more competitive. Here was the root of the problem. A stimulus to the centre might have had detrimental effects: 'almost every economist of note . . . drew attention to the dangers of monetary expansion feeding through into prices rather than employment' (Glynn and Booth, 1985, p. 93). This was already happening, even without artificial stimuli, as the economy moved towards the peak of the trade cycle in mid-decade, as Keynes himself recognized (Peden, 1980, p. 11). As for the reduction of export costs, it would have required a general wage-cutting campaign; not only would this have been politically difficult, but, if successful, it would also have cut working-class purchasing power and so reduced domestic demand, particularly for the products of the new industries which depended on the buoyancy of the home market.

In addition, the leading advocates of radical policies were not individuals from whom most people would have purchased a used car in the 1930s. Lloyd George, who had advocated proto-Keynesian policies at the 1929 election, and who in 1935 brought forward proposals for a 'New Deal', was distrusted, and his opposition to the National Government at the time of the 1931 election had set the final seal on his reputation as a pure opportunist and adventurer for many, particularly where it mattered: in governmental circles. Mosley, who advocated a massive increase in the economic role of the State in the 'Mosley Memorandum' of 1930, was seen widely, even before his move to Fascism, as, in the words of Baldwin, 'a cad and a wrong 'un'. And Keynes excited deep distrust, even on the Labour side, for his self-publicity in the 1920s and early 1930s; for his refusal to back the National Government in 1931 when its victory at the polls had been seen as the prerequisite of national survival; and for, as one senior Treasury official put it even in 1939, his 'customary over-optimism, over-emphasis and neglect of ulterior consequences' which suggested that 'he sets himself out to instil distrust in his readers' (Middleton, 1982, p. 73). These were not men whom government policy-makers were wont to take too seriously. More concretely, the 'radical' packages they put forward in the 1930s all had serious weaknesses — such as the issue of the trade balance and the problems of administration — which were never ironed out sufficiently to make their policies irresistible (Booth and Pack, 1985).

Nor did foreign examples provide easy solutions. On the left there was much enthusiasm for Soviet-style planning, which fed through into a more broadly-based 'planning' movement in Britain. For example Lord Lothian, a Liberal, wrote privately in 1931 of the need for 'a rough Gosplan' to solve Britain's difficulties (Thorpe, 1991, p. 61). On the right, after 1933, there was some admiration for the way Hitler seemed to be solving Germany's economic problems through state direction. There was also interest in Roosevelt's New Deal, while in 1937 the Labour leader, Attlee, waxed lyrical about the economic achievements of moderate left governments in Sweden and New Zealand (Attlee, 1949, pp. 31–3, 141). But these were not really solutions at all. For most of the decade, the economic situation in Britain was nowhere near so bad as to tempt policy-makers into adopting the drastic 'solutions' of Russia and Germany; New Zealand and Sweden were very different countries from Britain, especially in having fewer intractable economic difficulties; and in the USA the New Deal was more of a public relations exercise than a real economic success. Britain has been described as the only major Western industrial nation to reject deficit finance as a means of promoting recovery. It did not fare appreciably worse than its rivals because of it.

Nonetheless, the later 1930s has sometimes been seen as a period in which the Treasury abandoned, or at least modified, its 'view', and moved towards Keynesian strategies. The evidence usually cited for this is the deficit-financed rearmament programme, which began in 1937, and the plans drawn up for the public works which were to commence once intensive rearmament had been completed. But considerable caution is needed here, as suggested earlier. It had long been considered respectable to borrow in time of war, and therefore it was not a particularly revolutionary departure to finance, through deficits, a programme of rearmament in preparation for a war which, rhetoric about 'peace for our time' notwithstanding, most planners expected to occur. This was merely an extension of existing practice. Secondly, given that war was expected, the aim of the public-works scheme was less to promote peacetime employment than to develop infrastructure and prepare the workforce for the conflict. Contemporaries tended to believe that long periods of unemployment led to the deterioration of workers' abilities and initiative, so it made sense to rehabilitate them in this way.

It is also worth noting that the experience of rearmament reinforced many of the authorities' prejudices against public-works schemes. Underspending in the initial stages had buttressed the belief that there were massive difficulties in swiftly implementing a programme of heavy public expenditure, while the effects on employment were believed to be limited (Glynn and Howells, 1980, p. 36; Middleton, 1985, p. 121). Thus, it would seem that there was no wholesale conversion to Keynesianism in the later 1930s. It is also doubtful whether the experience of rearmament suggested that deficit-financed public works could have reduced unemployment substantially during the decade as a whole. The great advantage of rearmament over any other scheme to boost employment was its strong linkage to the depressed staple areas. No other project could have tackled structural unemployment in this way. A large-scale building programme, for example, would have exacerbated shortages of skilled labour and, at least from 1934 onwards, overheated the economy in the south and the Midlands, since they were the locations of the industries which would have benefited most. This in turn would have raised foreign exchange difficulties. And all this assumes, naively in view of the administrative difficulties outlined above, that such a programme could have been put into effect at all. In other words, rearmament was a one-off project, intended by the authorities as such, and carried no 'lessons' for the overall economic experience of Britain during the 1930s.

By and large, then, economic policy in the thirties, while innovative, still recognized the primacy of market forces and aimed to provide conditions in which private enterprise could flourish. Suggestions for radical alternatives were unconvincing and certainly the situation was never so bad that they had to be tried. Other policies might perhaps have improved matters, but it was at least as likely that they would have made a not intolerable macro-economic situation worse: and the first people to have suffered would have been those who were already hardest hit. Real life demanded, not the romantic

84

idealism of subsequent historians, but hard decisions about difficult problems. It is on that basis that the economic policy-makers should be judged.

CONCLUSION

The British economy in the 1930s moved from a depression which seemed shocking to contemporary observers, but which was mild by international standards, into a strong burst of prosperity in mid-decade and then, late in 1937, into a recession from which the escape was to be provided by massive state expenditure on rearmament. However, the problems were structural as well as cyclical, so that even at the peak of a quite impressive boom the staple industries remained depressed and unemployment, at 9 to 10 per cent, over one million. The economy was shifting in emphasis towards 'new' industries, which acted as subsidiaries to the building boom in reviving the economy after 1932; but even in 1938 the staple industries remained too significant a sector of the economy to be brushed aside. There was some restructuring, but it was partial.

In these circumstances, and with severe constraints facing it, government adopted more innovative policies than in the 1920s, but rejected radical departures, using the unemployment benefits system to relieve pressure on it to do more. In this it can be criticized for being unadventurous, but, given the scale of the problems faced, it probably did as well as could be expected in maintaining stability and promoting, or at least not retarding, prosperity in most parts of the country. If this is not an heroic assessment it is because the government's was not an heroic performance; but it was by no means the worst imaginable, and it is difficult to see a feasible policy which could have achieved appreciably better results.

85

4

Society

In recent years social history has joined, or even replaced, economics as the arena in which historians differ most significantly on the 1930s. These debates are wide-ranging and, in a work of this scale, can only be dealt with selectively. However, this chapter provides an attempt to address three related questions. First, how far was British society dominated by class divisions? Was life outside work — studied here in terms of housing and recreation — moving in directions which further split society? Next, did social policy work for all sections of society, or only for the better off? And finally, if there was improvement, why did the 1930s become a byword for misery and deprivation?

A CLASS-RIDDEN SOCIETY?

Class divisions were undoubtedly important in British society in the 1930s, and while there were other lines of cleavage, they were, in the main, diminishing in significance. It was not a time of aggressive class consciousness; and social status determined political allegiance more for the middle than for the working class. But, certainly later in the decade, there were signs that the working class was becoming more homogeneous while sections of the middle class were becoming more sympathetic towards aspects of working-class aspirations: thus was laid the basis, though only that, of the political change that was finally brought to light in Labour's electoral landslide of 1945.

It would not do to overstate the extent of social change before the Second World War. There still existed, at the apex of society, a tiny proportion of the population who could be characterized as 'an upper class'. Even here, though, there was something of a split between landed and non-landed wealth. In respect of the former, the period was not as grim as has sometimes been alleged, and landed society remained significant until the Second World War, despite high death duties. One reason for the survival of the older aristocratic families was that they had sold much of their land in the aftermath of the Great War, for by the 1930s agricultural rents had fallen to their lowest level since the 1870s. Those in a position to 'cash in' their assets thus fared well, and it was not so much the top aristocrats as the landed gentry, one step below, who suffered. The gentry tended to be even more dependent on falling agricultural rents for income. Some had to abandon their country houses; many more had to tighten their belts (although it was hardly into abject poverty that they fell). But the real money-makers were the newer, non-landed plutocrats, the most successful of whom, the shipowner and financier, Sir John Ellerman, left £37 million in 1933 (Rubinstein, 1981, p. 43). Although by far the most successful, he was only one of a number of people who, starting with little, became extremely rich. One should, in fact, say 'men' rather than 'people', since even the ten women who were millionairesses in their own right between the wars had inherited the money from men (Rubinstein, 1981, p. 250). One thing which the new plutocrats and the old aristocrats had in common, though, was their increasing reluctance to take a high-profile role in party politics. Those who took any overt interest confined themselves to financing the Conservative and, to a lesser extent, the Liberal National and New parties; the rest made 'a retreat into their enclosed and uncaring world' (Beard, 1989, p. 55).

This left the middle class to fill the political roles once taken up by their social 'betters'. Yet the middle class was, again, no straightforward or especially coherent body. Perhaps only in politics were they reasonably united, insofar as they tended overwhelmingly to support the National Government against the increasingly union- and often class-rhetoric-dominated Labour party. There were clashes, not only between the professional and business classes (4.6 and 10.4 per cent of the population respectively) (Routh, 1980, p. 5), but also, the some extent, within those groups. Professionals did not come from all walks of life; it was assuredly not a meritocratic society. Their backgrounds tended to be middle or lower-middle class, which was no surprise, given the poor condition of the state sector in education. Professional people rarely became rich, but they were respected, lived comfortably, and were secure from unemployment. Barristers were probably best off, but doctors who combined exploitation of the national health insurance panel scheme with private practice also fared very well (Digby and Bosanquet, 1988). But generalization is dangerous. A top city veterinary surgeon could earn £3,000 a year, but a rural vet could expect only between a fifth and a half that much. Similarly, solicitors and accountants with their own practices might be earning £2,000 a year by the time they were forty, but their salaried counterparts earned much less (Carr-Saunders and Wilson, 1933, p. 461). By the 1930s, as the scope of the state and local authorities increased, growing numbers of professionals were being employed in the public sector, but while the Permanent Secretary to the Treasury earned £3,500, others earned considerably less: male teachers, for example, earned a tenth of that (Routh, 1980, pp. 73, 70). Women made up a substantial part of the professional sector, but were confined very largely to 'traditional' roles in the lower professions, especially teaching and nursing.

Employers, managers, and administrators, meanwhile, constituted a sizeable business-oriented middle class. Their economic fortunes fluctuated to such an extent that it is difficult to make meaningful generalizations, but two things can be stated with confidence. First, the economic improvement experienced over most of the decade undoubtedly helped them considerably; second, their grim experiences between 1929 and 1932 made

88

them resolute supporters of the National Government and also rendered them more cautious regarding social and economic change, for fear that these might trigger a still worse depression. But of longer-term significance was the fact that, as industrial ownership passed from small to larger firms, and from individuals to shareholders, managers were becoming more important within the group. Women were again conspicuous by their absence: only 13 per cent of managers in 1931 were female (as opposed to 20 per cent in 1911 and 17 per cent in 1921), and restaurant management was the only sector where they formed a majority − as with the lower professions, something of a 'woman's area' (Routh, 1980, p. 23).

The middle class, then, was far from homogeneous. Locally-raised businessmen clashed with professionals who tended to be more mobile and who saw themselves as a somewhat alien national elite: they even spoke differently (Perkin, 1989, pp. 266−73). Similarly, there were conflicts within the 'professional sector'. Self-evidently, a wealthy vet who earned £3,000 a year had little in common with a teacher paid a tenth as much, and still less with a female nurse earning a third of that. But the division went deeper than mere inequality. The vet would send his children to private schools and would want to keep taxation as low as possible. The teacher in the state sector, however, would want to maintain his or her living standard through high public expenditure which, in turn, meant higher taxation, especially of the better-off. Thus there was a fundamental clash of interests between the private- and the public-sector professionals, while a minority of managers, at least, might come to see the potential benefits, in terms of job security, professionalization, and so on, which might accrue to them if their firms were nationalized. This process had not gone far in the 1930s, partly because the prevailing sense was still one of relief that the middle class had not gone under in the depression, and partly because the Labour Party was able to do little to convince them of the benefits of nationalization; but nonetheless, the potential for a serious split in the middle class was there (Perkin, 1989).

Always problematic in any discussion of class is the lower-middle class. Yet, with the expansion of the service sector during the decade, it was of growing importance. Most men in clerical work had secure, respected employment, with good pay, pensions and, for many, paid holidays. In 1935 their salaries varied between £200 and £350. Hence they could be earning more than some lower professionals. Women were paid less; although they might earn over £200 p.a., the average salary was around half that amount (Routh, 1980, p. 90). In addition, prospects for women to advance were slight, given that public authorities and many firms forced them to leave their jobs on marriage. But even male clerks did not have things all their own way all the time. The 1929–32 slump, in particular, hit many very hard indeed. Salaries were cut by up to 25 per cent; many firms reduced the number of automatic annual increments on their salary scales; working hours were often extended; and many were made redundant. It seems reasonable to state that 100,000 were out of work at the trough of the depression; but, since they were not covered by unemployment insurance, they could not claim unemployment benefit. Many had to take on hopeless jobs, for example as salesmen, where they might make a pound a week if they were lucky – a catastrophic fall in income (Klingender, 1934, pp. 85–97). Most remained in employment, though, and as the economy revived and the clerical sector expanded such problems were alleviated. At the same time, there was a shaking of some of the old certainties and a potential, perhaps not realized until 1945, for a change in the voting habits of a lifetime. But there is little evidence of this during the 1930s.

Yet for all that, the bulk of the population – three-quarters, in fact – was made up of manual workers. These workers, of course, were not a homogeneous bloc; far from it. They were divided, first, by industry; then, by their level of skill. Skilled workers constituted 26.7 per cent of the national workforce in 1931, semi-skilled 35.0 per cent, and unskilled, 14.8 per cent; the evidence of the 1951 Census would suggest that all three categories declined slightly during the thirties (Routh, 1980, p. 7). Women tended to be confined to the semi-skilled category (since they were barred from apprenticeships and unskilled jobs largely depended on physical strength) and they were generally paid less, partly as a result of the skill-level of their employment and partly because of prevailing views on gender roles. Within each industry, wages depended on skill. Differentials between skilled and other workers grew until about 1934, but thereafter they narrowed, especially in 1938–40. But economic fortunes overall were based to an even greater extent upon the industry in which a worker was engaged. Being skilled was no guarantee against unemployment, as thousands of unemployed coal-face workers could testify, while for those in work wages depended largely on the prosperity of the industry involved. A semi-skilled worker in a prosperous industry could earn more than a skilled worker employed in an ailing one, as table 4.1 demonstrates.

Real wages rose for manual workers in work, certainly until the later 1930s, when rising prices pulled them back a little. Taking 1850 as 100, real wages rose to 190 in 1913–14, 234 in 1924, and 354 in 1935, before falling back to 349 in 1939 as wage rises failed to keep pace with inflation. However, standards had only fallen very slightly, and the gains over the 1920s were still substantial (Benson, 1989, p. 55). It is difficult

TABLE 4.1 *Annual Earnings of Workers, 1935 (£)*

Type of worker	Highest earnings	Average	Lowest earnings
Skilled male	Railway engine drivers 258	197	Coalface workers 149
Semi-skilled male	Bus/tram drivers (London) 218	168	Railway platelayers 128
Unskilled male	Brewery workers (London) 162	136	Railway porters 114
Skilled female	Upholsterers 114	86	Pottery transferers 76
Semi-skilled female	Domestic servants 115	100	Clothing machinists 73
Unskilled female		73	

Source: G. Routh: *Occupation and Pay in Great Britain 1906–79* (1980), pp. 101–19

to disagree with Rubinstein that '[t]he "normal" working-class income was now, for possibly the first time in British history, above the subsistence level' (1986, p. 75).

This would suggest that there was some common experience among the working classes. Yet analysis of trade unionism cautions against seeing the working class as particularly homogeneous. First, and despite some amalgamations, there remained a plethora of organizations seeking to recruit members. Second, it is a misnomer to think of the unions themselves as a unified bloc. Finally, and most importantly of all, the level of unionization, though higher in Britain than anywhere else in the world, was not as high as one might think, although there was some progress here during the 1930s. By the late 1920s the 'poaching' of members of one union by another had been pretty well outlawed, and in 1939 the TUC's Bridlington Agreement prevented unions from trying to recruit in workplaces where more than half the membership already belonged to another union. Meanwhile, the proportion of the workforce unionized, which had fallen from 25.7 per cent in 1929 to 22.6 per cent in 1933 under the impact of economic depression, rose thereafter to 31.6 per cent in 1939. The fact that the rise was sustained through the recession of 1937–8 shows the continuing importance of the staple industries to the union movement as a whole; in the new manufacturing and service industries unions often lagged behind, despite the efforts of militant shop stewards (Cronin, 1984, pp. 243, 103–10). Even so, it was during the thirties that the foundations were laid for the advancement of unionization during and after the Second World War.

Unemployment, often seen as *the* characteristic of the decade, was another factor to affect some workers far more than others. It rose dramatically between 1929 and 1932, peaking in the latter year at 23 per cent of insured workers (probably 3.75 million were unemployed in all). Thereafter it fell, but never below 9 per cent (1.4 million), before the renewed recession of 1937–8; even subsequent recovery left it at over a million until 1940. Unemployed skilled workers often experienced the sharpest fall in living standards because benefits were set below unskilled wages to encourage people to take any job in preference to being out of work. But there was no unemployed 'class' as such. As a sympathetic researcher wrote at the end of the decade, people needed to 'reject the view that the unemployed [could] be described as a uniform mass of caps, grey faces, hands-in-pockets street-corner-men with empty stomachs on the verge of suicide, and only sustained by the hope of winning in the Pools, as utterly false' (Singer, 1940, p. 80). This is not to belittle the problems of the unemployed, but it is insulting to them to believe that the people affected faded away because of unemployment.

The national figures only tell half the story. There were, in particular, massive regional disparities. The majority of workers had no significant spell of unemployment between 1929 and 1940, and for many others their sole experience of it came before 1933. But for some, it was long-lived, especially in the areas dependent on the declining staple industries: Lancashire suffered with the cotton industry, and Tyneside with ship-building. Coal was worst-hit by economic problems, and although some areas, like Nottinghamshire, fared reasonably well, the overall picture in the mining industry was one of gloom. Unemployment remained high among miners throughout the decade, and even those in work were no longer well-paid compared with skilled workers in other industries. The problem was that mining tended to be heavily concentrated in south Wales, the north-east and east Midlands of England, Cumberland, Lancashire, Yorkshire, and central Scotland. Many of these regions were officially designated as Special Areas in 1935 because of the persistence of depression there even after the national economy as a whole had moved into prosperity, although, as has been seen, it did them little good. Thus by 1936, for example, one in four workers in the Rhondda, and almost one in five in Crook (County Durham) had been unemployed for a year or more (Pilgrim Trust, 1938, p. 15). The older and less-skilled workers were hit especially hard, having, as it seemed, little prospect of re-employment, and the survey literature of the decade is replete with comments such as that of the wife of a 62-year-old miner that they 'would both rather be dead than go on like this' (Beales and Lambert, 1934, p. 28).

There is no doubt that many of the unemployed suffered drab, debt-threatened lives. Yet, at the same time, they usually showed an impressive resilience. In the depressed areas, especially, people did not succumb to despair, partly because so many others were in the same position. In some ways, despair was more characteristic of those who could not find work in the more prosperous areas, who had less mutual support and who often felt guilty that they could not find a job (Singer, 1940, p. 103). People generally coped, helped by a benefits system which, though certainly not generous, did provide for the basics of life. And, of course, it bears repetition that for those in work these were years of unprecedented prosperity, in many ways anticipating the affluence of the 1950s. For example, the prosperity of the motor industry meant that places like Oxford and Coventry were characterized by high wages and regular employment. Derby prospered with the railway, Rolls-Royce, and artificial textiles. To some extent, voting patterns during the decade reflected some of these factors, with Labour polling far better in the declining staple areas than in the more prosperous new industry-dominated parts of the country, particularly the south-east and the west Midlands. It is noteworthy that Labour did not win a single seat in Birmingham in 1931 or 1935.

Thus there were clear regional divisions within the working class. But this was not a new phenomenon; and other non-class cleavages were becoming, perhaps, less significant. Religion had once crossed the class divide, but as adherence in the Nonconformist churches declined, the points of convergence between workers and their social 'betters' also diminished. Ethnicity has also been a potent force in masking class divisions for much of this century, but the 1930s were a time of no great ethnic tensions. The failure of Mosley's BUF to exploit racism successfully outside east London merely underscores the fact (see chapter 2). Similarly, this was, so far as most of Britain was concerned, a relatively peaceful time in Ulster, although IRA bombs in London in 1939 suggest that one

94

should not be too complacent; while in Scotland and Wales, the rise of nationalist parties did not go far and reflected more of a cultural renaissance than a force for real social division at this stage. Gender had also threatened to become a major issue in the past, but the inter-war period, and especially the thirties, saw a growing cult of domesticity; the idea of 'a woman's place' was subscribed to even by many feminists, like the MP Eleanor Rathbone. Even where there was a tradition of women working, such as in the textile industry in the north-west of England, women were deemed to require lower wages since their earnings essentially supplemented those of their husbands. The spread of household gadgets like vacuum cleaners could, theoretically, have freed more women to work outside the home, but, given the prevailing ideology, it simply meant that men and women expected higher standards of housework.

There were, then, no dramatic changes in the structure of British society in the 1930s. It was still a hierarchical society in which there were gross inequalities of wealth and opportunity. The later 1930s saw a resurgence in the number of estates of £100,000 or over which were sold off in the 'Indian summer' of the rich (Rubinstein, 1981, pp. 40–3). There was some redistribution of wealth, due to graduated taxation, death duties, and transfer payments to the poor, but this can be overstated: between 1924–30 and 1936–8 the share of total personal wealth owned by the top 1 per cent did fall, but only from 62 to 56 per cent, while the figure for the top 10 per cent fell still less, from 91 to 88 per cent (Perkin 1989, pp. 243–4). Redistribution was therefore as much from the very rich to the wealthy as from those two groups as a whole to the rest of the populace. Ellerman's wealth alone would have paid the un-employment assistance of 592,948 people for a year at 1936 rates. Yet even in the halcyon days of the welfare state after the Second World War, class still determined opportunity to a considerable extent, particularly as between the middle and working classes (Marwick, 1980, pp. 199, 207).

At the same time, though, certain changes were taking place. Patterns of deference were changing, for example, as the aris-tocracy withdrew from the public gaze and was replaced by new idols, especially Hollywood film stars (see below). And during this period there was also a shift in high social prestige from the old upper-class elites to those who had more 'professional' qualities (Cannadine, 1980, p. 425; Rubinstein, 1986, p. 39). The fact that the process of redistribution had begun at all encouraged those who wanted it to go further. And, while we may not accept fully the view that trade unions were becoming part of the state machinery, they had certainly acquired a legitimacy in official eyes which they had not possessed even a decade before (cf. Middlemas, 1979).

In the longer term, there was also the potential for two further developments. The first, already taking place during the decade, was the consolidation of the working class as such, as other lines of cleavage declined in importance and as the vicissitudes of capitalism suggested to increasing numbers the need for more collectivism. The second concerned the middle classes. During the 1930s they, too, were defensive: defending their privileges and status against the twin threats of the organized working class and a negative perception of 'socialism'. In 1945, many would hold fast to those views, but the thirties had a profound effect on a minority. Some, especially in the lower-middle class, were shaken from their old commitments by their experience of unemployment and stayed with the National Government primarily because of their negative perceptions of Labour. As Marwick has written, for parts of the decade 'the distinction between the upper-middle class and the lower-middle class was quite sharp' (Marwick, 1980, p. 182). And, although the point can be over-stressed, Bradley is probably right to argue that a 'sizeable and growing minority among the middle classes felt only guilt and embarrassment when they compared their relatively easy lives to those of others' (1982, p. 117). As prosperity increased, it became easier to argue that government could afford to spend more money to help the disadvantaged.

During the 1930s, then, class consciousness was largely defensive. The separate classes were not really dangerous, as they were in parts of Europe: there would be no Fascist or Communist takeover in Britain. In part, of course, this reflected the fact that, for those in work — the overwhelming majority — real incomes were rising for most of the period. But by the end of the decade growing numbers of the middle classes were looking for a more dynamic alternative to the pragmatic plodding of the National Governments. The Second World War provided this, first by shaking long-standing perceptions, secondly by creating conditions in which idealism became fashionable, and finally by transforming the Labour Party and people's perceptions of it. Thus were laid the foundations of a new departure in British politics: that it came in the form of the Labour victory in 1945 owed most to events after 1939.

DOMESTICATION AND 'PRIVATIZATION'? HOUSING AND LEISURE

Improved living standards were also reflected in the changing nature of home life during the decade. Developments in both housing and leisure made for a more domesticated and private lifestyle for increasing numbers of people. This in turn had some effect on the solidity or otherwise of social classes; but it also left an image of the thirties as a rather selfish period in British history.

The nature and extent of housing changed considerably during the inter-war years. The 1930s saw extensive construction, considerable slum clearance, and a growth in both public-sector and owner-occupied housing at the expense of the private-rented sector. In addition, houses themselves became more comfortable; that, in turn, contributed to a growth of the cult of domesticity and the increasing 'privatization' of culture and leisure patterns.

Most of the boom in residential construction comprised privately-built housing for sale to owner-occupiers. Between the wars, almost 4 million new houses were built, 2.9 million of them for sale. The greater part of this construction took place in the 1930s; in 1935—9 alone, 1.6 million new houses were built (Burnett, 1978, pp. 242—6). Merrett has estimated that by 1939 32 per cent of houses were owner-occupied, as opposed to 10 per cent in 1914 (1982, p. 16). Owner-occupation was not a new phenomenon, even if the figure of 10 per cent for 1914 is very speculative indeed. Before the Great War, some relatively prosperous working-class communities in, for example, south Wales, had had no alternative but to build their own houses, and sufficient income and support networks to enable them to do so. Newer middle-class suburbs had also been constructed on this basis. But a number of factors combined to expand this sector from the start of our period. Demographic change promoted demand in an already under-supplied housing market, with more people marrying at an early age and having smaller families. At the same time, older people were living longer, and real incomes rose. Supply constraints were eased, with cheap primary materials and inexpensive labour combined with cheap land (often opened up by transport development – cars and the extension of the London Underground allowed people to live further from their place of work) enabling speculative builders to cut their costs. Cheap money, in the form of low interest rates from 1932 onwards helped to sustain, even if it did not initiate, the boom. In addition, the evolution of building societies from 'quasi-philanthropic local institutions into national financial intermediaries' greatly facilitated mortgages, which underpinned the whole process (Humphries, 1987, p. 329). Finally, the entrepreneurial flair of speculative builders, who were prepared to operate on relatively narrow profit margins, maintained the supply. It is also worth noting, of course, that around a quarter of pre-1914 housing, previously rented, passed into owner-occupation during the interwar period as a whole.

These owner-occupiers, moving into their largely semi-detached homes in 'ribbon developments' along main roads or on suburban estates with quaint rural street names, were not a typical cross-section of the population. Owner-occupation could be found all over the country, but was especially strong in industrial towns, like Burnley in Lancashire and Newport in south Wales, with a tradition of working-class owner-occupation; in boom towns like Oxford and Coventry; and in towns which had a substantial middle-class presence, like Birmingham,

Norwich, or Hastings. Overall, higher levels of owner-occupation were to be found in the south, and the more prosperous areas of the Midlands, than elsewhere. This reflected the fact that owner-occupiers were more middle-class than the population as a whole. Leeds saw a quadrupling in the proportion of working-class owner-occupation (Finnigan, 1980, p. 134), but the generally higher and more regular incomes of the middle classes made them better able to obtain and afford mortgages. Thus, by the later 1930s, 55 per cent of owner-occupiers were middle-class, as opposed to 19 per cent who were working-class (Swenarton and Taylor, 1985, p. 391). Given the larger proportions of working-class people in the much smaller number of owner-occupiers before 1914, it can even be claimed that owner-occupation became more middle-class.

The working class, in fact, continued to be housed predominantly in private-rented accommodation, which still accounted for 58 per cent of housing in 1938. However, this was a significant drop from the 90 per cent of 1914 (Merrett, 1982, p. 16). As slum-clearance legislation took hold in the 1930s, much of this accommodation was swept away, to be replaced by local authority housing. Property had, in any case, become a less sound investment for landlords after 1915, when wartime inflation had forced the government to adopt rent controls; although this had been intended as a temporary step, it had had to be extended on repeated occasions after the cessation of hostilities. By 1933, two-thirds of rents were still subject to 'controls', and the National Government, for all its commitment to free enterprise and the market, could not contemplate their removal − a point which must qualify claims that their philosophy was dominated by the needs of the *rentier* class (Daunton, 1984, p. 15; McKibbin, 1990, pp. 259−93). Rent controls meant less income for the landlords, which in turn meant less money to reinvest; inevitably, therefore, the standard of private-rented accommodation declined.

Local authority housing stepped into the breach. Labour's 1924 Housing Act had boosted public housing construction, by increasing government subsidies to councils. Their 1930 Act then offered subsidies to councils for slum clearance and the construction of replacement housing. The National Government accepted the latter, but believed that private enterprise should be responsible for 'general need' housing, and so subsidies under the 1924 Act were terminated in 1933. Councils could now only receive financial help for slum clearance, which meant 'a return to a sanitary policy of public housing' (Daunton, 1984, p. 14). In 1935, the abatement of overcrowding was also deemed worthy of subsidy. By 1938, there seemed to have been considerable advances, and one-tenth of houses were owned by local authorities (Merrett, 1982, p. 16). During the inter-war period as a whole, over a million council houses were built. These houses tended to be far superior to the houses they replaced, being brighter, airier, and easier to clean, and having more bedrooms and better sanitary facilities.

It was not all good news. In quantitative terms the advance was rather slight. Local authorities demolished almost as many houses as they built between 1930 and 1939. In Scotland, in particular, overcrowding remained a problem of massive proportions, with 22.5 per cent of houses overcrowded in 1935−6, as opposed to just 3.8 per cent in England (Royle, 1987, p. 31). Secondly, rents proved to be a problem. A survey of Sheffield in 1930 found that the higher rents on a new council estate had forced around 30 per cent of those rehoused since 1926 to return to lower-rent, slum accommodation (Owen, 1931, p. 41). Although this related to the depression period, the high rents continued into the thirties. By 1938, 80 per cent of Bristol council's rents were too expensive for around a third of the city's working-class population (Dresser, 1984, p. 209); and in Stockton-on-Tees, it was found that dietary deficiencies resulting from the payment of higher rents were leading to a higher death rate on the council estates than in the slums. However, local authorities were in a tight spot. If rents were reduced generally, they would have less money for new building. Whitehall's preferred solution was for councils to operate differential rents, subsidizing poorer tenants' rents by charging better-off tenants more. But this would have aroused considerable hostility from tenants on the grounds, first, that it would involve some form of means-testing; and, secondly, that the better-off tenants would have been subsidizing the rest. Even so, some rebate schemes were started.

There was also some criticism of the type of houses built. Those constructed without parlours, for example, offended traditions of working-class 'respectability' which demanded a 'best room'. Perhaps more importantly, the sprawling, low-density estates tended to lack amenities, not just libraries, churches, shops, and meeting-halls, but also public houses, which were often excluded deliberately. Furthermore, there was a loss of community. In Sheffield it was found that some tenants on the new estate 'sentimentalize[d] about the lost society of the [slum] courts and the neighbourliness of congested streets' (Owen, 1931, p. 41). More than that, the extended family was often stretched to, and beyond, breaking-point, placing new burdens on young and old alike. Something of a social service vacuum emerged, and it was not one with which most local authorities were equipped or inclined to deal; often 'tenants were informed of the social behaviour which was required of them by the Council through the issue of handbooks, the exclusion of publicans, and the encouragement of gardening' (Daunton, 1984, p. 25). But this degree of social control was mild indeed when compared with that prevailing in the new colliery towns of the Dukeries coalfield in Nottinghamshire, where what amounted to a company police force patrolled the estates (Waller, 1983, pp. 98–9).

Improved standards of construction, technological advance, and rising prosperity also meant that many people had a more comfortable home life. By 1939, 75 per cent of houses were wired for electricity; 80 per cent of such houses had an electric iron and 30 per cent a vacuum cleaner (Burnett, 1978, p. 256). These amenities did not necessarily make the lives of those who had them any easier, owing to the prevailing ethos of 'the woman's place'; but it is certainly true to say that with improved living standards, and perhaps to some extent because of the extra cost of living in debt to a building society or paying a higher rent to the council, people were more inclined to spend

101

their evenings, at home, especially since there was now more to do there — including listening to the radio. Domesticity and its accompanying materialism had arrived.

This point is amply confirmed by reference to changing patterns of leisure during the decade. In fact, this was one of the most significant aspects of British society in the 1930s. There were three preconditions for the expansion of leisure pursuits: time, money, and provision, and all were present to an unprecedented degree. First, working hours had fallen dramatically immediately after the First World War, the average working week for a male manual worker being reduced from 54 hours in 1914 to 48 hours in 1919. While the gains made thereafter were unimpressive (47.7 hours in 1938), leisure provision in the thirties was catching up with the increased spare time made available to workers in the post-war period (Jones, 1986, pp. 16–17). In addition, the number of workers entitled to a week's paid holiday rose from 1 million in 1920 and 4 million in 1937, to 11 million in 1939, partly as a result of the Holidays with Pay Act, 1938 (Perkin, 1989, p. 282). Secondly, more money was available because of increased real wages and reduced expenditure on drink (see below). Finally, there was an increase in leisure provision, by voluntary organizations, local authorities (combining a desire to 'improve' their citizens with a desire to win their votes), and, most importantly, private enterprise, which saw leisure as a 'growth industry'. The sheer expansion of the range and output of leisure activities must temper, or even destroy, any view that the thirties was a decade of depression. In addition, though, it should be noted that the areas of relative growth and decline made considerable comment on the broader development of British society.

The leisure pursuits which were in decline were the classic communal activities of the nineteenth century: drinking and organized religion. It would, of course, be rash to overplay the decline of the former. A survey of Bolton towards the end of the decade found that 'more people spen[t] more time in public houses than they d[id] in any other buildings except private houses and workplaces' (Mass-Observation, 1943, p. 17). But drink seemed to be losing its grip on hearts and

102

pockets: York, where less, and weaker, beer was being consumed in fewer and fewer pubs was certainly typical (Rowntree, 1941, pp. 472–3). Some brewers, like Mitchell's and Butler's in Birmingham, were keen to update their image; car parks and lounge bars without spittoons aimed at a more affluent clientele of both men and women. Yet this could not fully compete with the advance of cinemas and dance-halls, both of which were increasingly important; and one result of this female encroachment on the formerly male preserve was an expansion of working-men's clubs, which often excluded women.

Similarly, churchgoing also declined, certainly in the case of the Protestant denominations. Nonconformity was hardest hit. The proportion of Methodists in the population fell by almost 7.5 per cent in the seven years up to the outbreak of war in 1939 (Currie et al., 1977, p. 66). The Anglican Church fared better, but attendance still declined slightly. The various Protestant sects built very few churches during the decade. It was true that around 10 per cent of the adult population now listened to services broadcast by the BBC (Currie et al., 1977, p. 235) but, even so, Rowntree felt that 'the influence of the Churches [was] weaker than at any time in the memory of those now living' (Rowntree, 1941, p. 476). General disillusionment with religion, and the growth of doubt, helped explain this; so, too, did the failure of the Protestant Churches to give a very clear lead (Bebbington, 1989, pp. 181–228). In addition, religion ceased to be very significant politically, and the churches' social-service functions were largely taken over by public authorities. Most important of all, perhaps, was the fact that churches no longer provided the best cheap entertainment available. Newer leisure pursuits were more exciting and fashionable, and, as respect for the Sabbath declined, they were increasingly in direct conflict with religion. Even believers now found less time to attend church; they would rather be out rambling, motoring, or visiting relatives, or at home gardening, reading, or listening to the wireless (McLeod, 1984, p. 66). The Catholic Church, though, continued to prosper. There were around 3 million Catholics in Britain, heavily concentrated in a few areas such as the north-west of England,

Tyneside, London, south Wales and west-central Scotland. Perhaps this concentration, and something of a 'siege mentality', helped to explain their resilience, shown by the increasing number of priests and a 14 per cent increase in the number of churches (Currie et al., 1977, p. 213). But the Catholics were an exceptional minority.

Other old recreations were better-placed to retain their appeal. Sport was a case in point. Playing games became more widespread, assisted by municipal provision of facilities. By 1939 around 10,000 clubs were affiliated to county Football Associations (Mason, 1989, p. 149). For the elite, hunting continued to appeal, and newer sports, like aviation, were added. Meanwhile, spectator sports retained and, if anything, increased their popularity. Football crowds were larger than ever. Manchester City, on their way to winning the FA Cup in 1934, were watched by 72,841 people in the fifth round as they beat Sheffield Wednesday at Hillsborough, and then by 84,569 at their own ground as they beat Stoke City in the quarter-finals. The New Year fixtures between Rangers and Celtic in Glasgow attracted 92,000 in 1938 and 118,567 in 1939 (Rollin, 1980, pp. 327, 227, 514, 562). Cricket was followed avidly by all classes in England; in south Wales, rugby union dominated; while in parts of Lancashire and Yorkshire, rugby league continued to be popular. Newer sports, like speedway, and older ones, like boxing, also attracted a considerable following. The former Cabinet minister, J. H. Thomas, was not far wrong when he wrote in 1937: 'I think I know what lies close to the heart of the British public − sport!' (1937, p. 290). And Thomas's own career showed how the cross-class appeal of sport could increase social cohesion.

Closely related to sport was gambling, with bets totalling up to £400 million a year being staked throughout the 1930s. Horse-racing remained popular in this respect, but was being challenged by two newer developments. Greyhound racing had been introduced in the 1920s, and by 1931 there were seventeen tracks in London alone: ironically enough, some Labour MPs defeated in that year's general election took jobs promoting the sport. Meanwhile, football pools became

104

incredibly popular. By the late 1930s, the companies had ten million people on their books (McKibbin, 1990, pp. 107–10). Stakes of 2s6d (12½p) could bring prizes as high as £22,000 – almost a hundred times the annual earnings of the best-paid manual workers (Royle, 1987, p. 269). Some saw this as a sign of deep moral decay, but they were wrong. Most working people gambled, and most did not impoverish their families, or end up destitute. Gambling was popular because it offered excitement, gave people an intellectual challenge of a nature acceptable to mainstream working-class culture, and was a key aspect of working-class budgeting. Gambling, in fact, showed the abilities, resilience and resourcefulness of the British working class.

Hobbies of all kinds flourished in the 1930s, when more time and, usually, money could be devoted to them than ever before. As George Orwell wrote in 1941, there was 'an addiction to hobbies and spare-time occupations' in 'a nation of stamp-collectors, pigeon-fanciers, amateur carpenters, coupon-snippers, darts-players, crossword-puzzle fans' (1970, pp. 77–8). Music remained popular in middle-class and better-off working-class household; but it was more likely to be played on a gramophone than a piano; and, as with all things, those who were better off could afford the better-quality machines. Gardening became more popular as the opportunities for it increased, with more houses being built with gardens and the provision of allotments by local authorities. As houses became more comfortable, home-centred hobbies generally became more popular; women, freed somewhat from more traditional chores by labour-saving devices, could take up crochet or knitting, safely within their allotted 'sphere'.

One ancient pastime to retain its appeal was sex. Traditionally, the thirties have been seen as a time of reaction against the sexual licence of the 'roaring twenties', but too much can be made of this. The 1920s had not been very liberated for most people. Then again, the thirties saw the publication of literature which stressed the importance of sexual pleasure for both partners within marriage. But marriage was the operative word, and remained the basis of conventional morality, notwithstanding the fact that divorce was made somewhat easier in 1937. Even so, pre- and extra-marital sex continued to thrive and was probably easier to obtain: certainly prostitution was in decline. Casual sex was facilitated by the increasing availability and reliability of artificial contraceptives, although the withdrawal method was widely practised among sections of the working class in particular. In Bolton, as in countless other towns, the narrow backstreet alleys, in which the streetlights were extinguished at 11.15 p.m., afforded the ideal venue for a 'knee-trembler' (Mass-Observation, 1943, p. 267; Calder and Sheridan, 1984, p. 49). However, it would not do to overstate promiscuity. One summer in the late thirties, twenty-three Mass-Observation investigators visited Blackpool, 'expect[ing] to see copulation everywhere'. This was a somewhat fanciful expectation, but even if not taken literally, they were to be sorely disappointed. Despite extensive and intrepid efforts, including pretending to be drunk late at night on the beach and falling on to courting couples 'to feel what they were doing exactly', they 'scored only four records of copulation', and one of them was by an Observer who, perhaps, did it out of duty. One interesting finding was that women took the initiative in 65 per cent of 'pick-ups' (Calder and Sheridan, 1984, pp. 51−9). Yet for many people, little if anything changed. In particular, homosexuality remained illegal and risky; to take but two examples, the writer, Harold Nicolson, was forced to resign from the Foreign Office, and the Liberal politician, Lord Beauchamp, had to flee the country, when it looked as though they were going to be exposed.

Some people went to Blackpool in search of sex, but this was not the only reason for the increasing popularity of holidays in the 1930s. The very wealthy could still afford to 'winter' abroad, but foreign travel remained an elite pursuit: significantly, of five leading politicians of all parties on vacation when the financial crisis broke in the summer of 1931, only Baldwin was out of the country. For the masses, paid holidays gave many people the time and money required, although it would not do to overstate this: only one in three could, or chose to, afford a holiday (Perkin, 1989, p. 282). By 1939 there were two hundred holiday camps in Britain, with those of Billy Butlin at Skegness and Clacton taking pride of place. Voluntary holiday organizations like the Camping Club of Great Britain more than doubled in membership during the decade (Jones, 1986, p. 64). A parallel, and perhaps more widespread, development was the rise of the 'day out' − the better-off driving into the countryside or to the coast in their cars (the number registered increased five-fold to 1.8 million between 1922 and 1937), and the rest taking advantage of special coaches or trains (Jones, 1986, pp. 21, 195). Cycling grew more popular among the working class as bicycles became relatively cheap; the rambling craze led ultimately to the designation of the National Parks after the Second World War.

But perhaps the most significant leisure development of the decade was the 'mass communications revolution', which had four aspects: cinema, wireless, the press, and literature. The first sound film had arrived in Britain in 1929, and from then onwards the cinema increased still further in popularity. By 1934 there were over 4,000 cinemas in Britain with almost 4 million seats and a weekly average attendance of 18.5 million (Rowson, 1934; Pronay, 1971). By 1939 the weekly figure had risen to 20 million (Richards, 1983, p. 32). New cinemas were always opening, and many were quite luxurious. The films offered attractions − excitement, escapism, and so on − but so too did the cinemas. They were places where working-class and, increasingly but still to a lesser extent, middle-class couples could go without the qualms raised for some by the pub, while their warmth and darkness had obvious appeal for courting couples. Some moralists objected, naturally, but they suffered a major defeat in 1932 when, after a period of confusion, local authorities were empowered to allow cinemas to open on Sundays. With even the middle class now attending this formerly working-class preserve in increasing numbers, politicians realized that cinemagoers were a lobby not to be offended. Among young people, certainly, only the rapidly-expanding (and under-researched) dance-halls rivalled the cinema. Cinema was democratizing in its effects: as well as providing a common experience to all classes, it also provided, in film stars, a new

107

focus for deference and admiration much more exciting than the aristocracy.

Cinema's appeal was matched in the home by the success of the wireless. By 1932, 43 per cent of households, including almost 20 million people, had a radio; by 1939 these figures had risen to 75 per cent and 34 million (Pegg, 1979, p. 32). Within Britain the British Broadcasting Corporation (BBC) had a monopoly. Its Director-General until 1937, Sir John Reith, hoped to use radio to 'uplift' the British people, but he was not particularly successful: by 1934 the BBC was broadcasting more light music and comedy than any other major station in Europe. In any case, people could always tune to foreign-based stations, like Radio Luxembourg, if they wanted things like the Littlewood's Pools Programme (Curran and Seaton, 1985, p. 134). But whatever the idiosyncracies of individual taste, the broader implication of the spread of radio was that social life was becoming more home-based during the 1930s.

Another aspect of the same process was the growth of the press. The interwar period saw the extension of the habit of newspaper-reading to the working class, and circulation figures reflected this. By 1939 19,460,000 newspapers a day were being sold, as opposed to 17,950,000 in 1930 and 14,670,000 in 1920 (Seymour-Ure, 1975, p. 236). Within those figures, there remained a distinction between the low-sale, up-market 'quality' papers, like *The Times*, and more sensational popular dailies like the *Daily Express*. However, both types of newspaper relied primarily on advertising for funding, and so circulation mattered most in terms of its ability to attract advertisers. Hence it seemed justifiable to spend large sums of money on attracting new readers, and the readers themselves could benefit. Competitions, with prizes of up to £5,000, were one means of increasing circulation. In addition, armies of canvassers toured the country offering people insurance and all kinds of free gifts if they would register as readers of their newspaper. 'A whole Welsh family, it was rumoured, could be clothed from head to toe for the price of eight weeks reading of the *Daily Express*' (Seymour-Ure, 1975, p. 249). Complete sets

108

of Dickens's works were another 'attraction'. In 1937, the typical popular daily employed five times as many canvassers as editorial staff (Curran and Seaton, 1985, p. 61). Newspapers also had to become more 'entertaining' and less 'educational' to maximize their readership.

Another development was the continuing decline of the provincial press; in other words, in England and Wales at least, the London-based 'national' press was becoming more and more dominant. Even provincial papers were increasingly being taken over by national 'chains', further diminishing diversity. Finally, new journals came on to the market to cater for hitherto under-exploited areas of readership and/or because of technological developments — thus, on the one hand, the introduction of more women's magazines, like *Secrets*, and children's comics like *Beano* and *Dandy*, and, on the other, the rise of pictorial journalism with *Picture Post*, launched in 1938.

Finally, more books were read in Britain in the 1930s than in any previous decade. More people could countenance reading books as the quality of literacy rose, a process assisted by the expansion of the popular press. At the same time, technological advances and the enterpreneurial flair of men like Allen Lane, who founded Penguin Books in 1936, and Victor Gollancz, who set up the Left Book Club in the same year, meant that good books could now be bought cheaply. The first Penguins, for example, sold for 6d (2½p), the same price as a packet of cigarettes. Meanwhile, local authorities were increasing public library provision dramatically. Whereas 85.7 million books had been issued by Britain's public libraries in 1924, by 1939 the figure had risen to 247.3 million (Jones, 1986, p. 97). While it would be naive to believe that most people were reading books which were intellectually demanding, the decade ended with the public better-informed than ever before, not least about their poorer compatriots. And, once again, the growth of reading reflected the privatization of leisure activity.

In the sphere of leisure, then, five processes were at work. First, secularization continued apace, reflected, for example, in the decline of organized religion and the Sunday opening of cinemas. There was, secondly, a diversification of leisure

109

pursuits. Thirdly, access to them was broadened by rising real incomes for those in work. At the same time, the thirties saw a society whose leisure was increasingly private, with the decline of pub and chapel, and the growth of home-based pursuits. Even the cinema was, in a sense, a private experience in that it was not a place where conversation was encouraged. Finally, there was something of a 'nationalization' process at work, with people travelling more, and watching the same films and, increasingly, reading the same newspapers and books the country over. Both integration and disintegration can be seen, therefore, in home life in the 1930s.

HEALTH, WELFARE, AND SOCIAL POLICY

Much of the above suggests that Britain was a society enjoying unprecedented levels of prosperity during the 1930s. Yet this was also, as we have seen, the time of the Jarrow March, of massive long-term unemployment, and the publication of books like Walter Greenwood's *Love on the Dole* (1933) and George Orwell's *The Road to Wigan Pier* (1937). In the areas of health and social policy, in particular, the governments of the 1930s have been hammered by their critics. But the policies of this decade were bound to look rather pale in comparison with the welfare state which emerged from the Labour victory of 1945. It is a central plank of the pessimists' argument regarding the 1930s that the health and welfare of substantial sections of the population were not only bad, but also worse than they need have been and, in some cases, actually deteriorating. The optimists, on the other hand, claim there was a general improvement, partly deriving from natural forces but also helped by the policies adopted by central and local government.

Government policy from 1931 onwards was based upon expediency rather than idealism. It aimed to restrict expenditure so that taxes could be kept low and the national budget balanced. To the latter end, it tried to shift some financial burdens to the local authorities. However, it centralized the one issue, unemployment relief, which was too controversial for local

110

government to continue handling. The benefits system was preserved, partly for political and partly for humanitarian reasons, but government was keen to maintain the principle of 'less eligibility' by keeping benefits at a low level. It was firmly committed to selective, rather than universal, provision, to which end, firstly, the insurance principle was retained regarding health and unemployment benefits, and, secondly, means tests were introduced for most personal social services. Finally, and following on from all this, the National Governments were extremely reluctant to introduce new schemes or undertake big new commitments.

The official figures certainly suggested that this was not an altogether unsuccessful strategy. United Kingdom infant mortality, for example, fell from 76 per 1,000 live births in 1929 to 55 per 1,000 in 1938 (HMSO, 1940, p. 44). Maternal mortality, also, was falling, at least from 1936. On this basis, Winter argues that 'the 1930s must be seen, ... despite the stubborn survival of pockets of terrible deprivation, as a period of major improvement of the health of mothers and infants of Britain' (1979, p. 462).

On what might such an improvement have been based? Improved diet was one factor. The 1930s saw increased consumption of eggs, milk, and fruit because of the lower prices of primary foods, the development of canning and refrigeration, publicity about nutrition, and the advertising campaigns of the agricultural marketing boards set up by the National Government. Better medical care was another factor. Scientific advances, like the introduction of the sulphonamide drugs, and advances in chemotherapy after 1936, also helped. Secondly, there was some advance in the health services available. The better-off could afford private treatment in increasing numbers, but there was a more general improvement in, for example, the hospital sector. The Conservatives' Local Government Act, 1929, allowed local authorities to convert Poor Law infirmaries into general hospitals admitting members of all classes. This meant a very significant development: the potential for the creation of 'a hospital system which relied neither on charity nor on the Poor Law' (Crowther, 1988, p. 73). Meanwhile,

111

voluntary hospitals co-operated more closely with local authorities in return for greater government financial assistance.

By 1937 some spectacular advances in health provision had been made in the public sector, especially in London, where the County Council had acquired 63 general hospitals, with 42,000 beds and 20,000 staff. As in some other big cities, the municipal hospitals were now of such a standard that they were competing seriously with the voluntary sector for paying, private patients (Fox, 1986, pp. 55–61). The voluntary hospitals were also thriving to such an extent that they could build and renovate on a considerable scale. The approach of war, which was expected to produce civilian casualties on a massive scale, promoted the creation of an emergency hospital service embracing all the nation's hospitals and ultimately forming the basis of the National Health Service in 1948. There were some improvements for panel patients (those covered by national health insurance) in general practice. For example, the doctor : patient ratio improved until 1937, when an extension of the scheme to young workers − who thereby benefited − reversed the trend.

Facilities for maternal and child welfare grew rapidly. In the 1930s such centres expanded to cover the majority of mothers in the country. Similarly, the number of midwives rose by over a third between 1928 and 1936, and legislation in the latter year required local authorities to employ an adequate number of full-time midwives (Winter, 1979, p. 459). Certainly in the area of childbirth, this brought improvements. While home remained the normal place of delivery, the proportion of institutional deliveries rose, and home delivery became safer given the improvements in antenatal care and the greater likelihood of the presence of a midwife at the birth.

Thirdly, the legacy of improved environmental conditions since the 1900s was making itself felt, while better housing could also be seen as a factor improving health. Rising real incomes for the majority also seem to have had a positive effect. It was now easier to feed one's family well, to afford better housing, and, in the case of the middle class, to afford private health insurance. State benefits also made some contribution to the nation's health. While it would be absurd to argue that they were particularly generous, they did help 'to separate deprivation from destitution' (Winter, 1983, p. 252). The later 1920s had seen a gradual extension of benefits, but financial crisis after 1930 led to a process of restriction which had three results: a general reduction of benefits (like unemployment benefit, cut by 10 per cent); disqualification of some types of worker from some types of benefit (Labour's 1931 'Anomalies' Act barred married women from claiming unemployment benefit); and the imposition of a means test on most personal social services and benefits. The idea, though, remained that everyone could claim something, somehow; and, if the worst came to the worst, people still had recourse to the Poor Law. The benefits were low, but they were better than nothing.

All this would seem to indicate a fairly rosy picture of the state of the nation's health in the 1930s. But a number of critics have suggested otherwise. The 'pessimists' claim, first, that the infant mortality figures are not all that impressive. Webster has argued that, taken over the long term, the 1930s represent 'a drag in the downward trend' (1982, p. 123), while Mitchell suggests that the rate, especially in Scotland, was higher than it should have been when compared with the situation prevailing in other developed countries (1985, p. 107). Secondly, the critics point to high rates of maternal mortality: in 1933 and 1934 these were higher than at the turn of the century, although even Webster is forced to admit that they fell thereafter (1982, p. 117). Thirdly, it has been argued that the national averages masked massive regional disparities. Finally, the pessimists take issue with the statistics themselves. The practice of the Conservative government of the 1980s – to which they were, without exception, passionately opposed – in terms of continually redefining the unemployment figures, informed their outlook here. There is some substance in the charges: the National Government did want to ensure that, if the figures erred, it was on the low side. But it is much more difficult to sustain an argument which suggests that the 1930s figures are grossly misleading. The charge has some substance, but it fails to test whether such practices were unique to the thirties, or common to all governments. It seems likely that the latter is true, and that therefore the figures, even if inaccurate in detail, are still an accurate reflection of a downward trend.

That said, a number of problems with the optimists' case remain. Firstly, there was growing evidence, as the decade progressed, that significant numbers of people were under-nourished. In 1934, 52 per cent of men attending army recruit-ment offices were below the required physical standard; four years later, a survey revealed that malnutrition was a direct cause of the death of up to 3,200 women per annum in child-birth (Mayhew, 1988, pp. 460, 455). In 1936 the nutritionist John Boyd Orr suggested that only half the country was so well-nourished that no improvement was called for, while one-fifth of children were chronically undernourished. Even under the less rigorous minima laid down by the British Medical Association, it was estimated that 8 million people were so poor that they could not afford an adequate diet (Webster, 1982, p. 121). Certainly, the increased consumption of fruit and dairy products seems to have benefited mainly the better-off (Mayhew, 1988, p. 459), while increased use of tobacco and convenience foods arguably did little to improve health, even if it did suggest rising prosperity. And, as the decade drew to a close, rising food prices and, for some, rents, at a time when benefits were not increased, did little to ease matters. Local authorities' efforts, like school meal provision, could be desultory, and of little real help to the needy.

Similarly, benefits have been much criticized. They were certainly not over-generous; the means test did demean many people, and could have deleterious effects on family life; the administrators could be insulting in their behaviour. In many distressed areas the unemployed had to make some use of the Poor Law machinery. Yet there was little uniformity in attitudes. A 1943 survey found that most people viewed the benefits system with 'a mixture of suspicion and grudging respect' (Harris, 1983, p. 208). It is a gross exaggeration to claim that local administrators generally had a 'punitive attitude' towards the poor (Webster, 1985, p. 227). Means tests were more uniformly disliked but some people, at least, who objected to the test being applied to themselves accepted the general need for some form of safeguard, as was the case with the equally unpopular rent rebate schemes.

Claims that there were great advances in medical care during the decade should be treated, perhaps, with caution. In general practice, private patients got a better deal than panel patients, and the doctors got a better deal than either (Digby and Bosanquet, 1988). The panel system gave doctors a flat rate fee per patient, which discouraged specialization by GPs; this, in turn, meant that people with anything beyond a fairly limited range of complaints had to be hospitalized, and since national health insurance did not cover such fees, patients had to pay themselves unless they qualified for help under the means test. The record of the maternity and child welfare clinics should also be viewed with caution. Their role was strictly circumscribed, and while most women and young children were attending the clinics by 1935, the extent to which they benefited remains an open question: maternal disablement continued to be stubbornly high. The main problem here was financial: the centres had to be financed by local authorities, and this meant that they were best-provisioned in prosperous areas, and most rudimentary in depressed areas. Attempts to subsidize local authorities for this work under the Special Areas legislation were rejected by the Cabinet. In addition, despite the movement of medical opinion during the decade towards the immunization of children against, for example, diphtheria, nothing was done about this, partly for fear of over-extending the state medical sector (Lewis, 1986, pp. 167–72).

One of the major reasons, indeed, for the discrepancies in standards of health was the continuation of a high level of local authority control. The State was concerned to push financial burdens back on to local authorities and away from the high-profile national budget. Yet this tended to reinforce disadvantage. At one stage, for example, the rate in Pontypridd was 23s11d (119p) in the pound, whereas in Oxford it was only 7s4d (36p). This made it far easier for the latter to improve its services, but the irony was that, because it was

115

prosperous, it had far less need to do so. In terms of nutritional supplementation, Rhondda Urban District spent £112 per thousand of population in 1935, whereas, two valleys away, Mountain Ash UD spent only £64 (Webster, 1985, p. 228, 223). School meals were often worst, or non-existent, in depressed areas where they were most needed, and the same was true of hospitals. The great majority of authorities who took over Poor Law hospitals were in the larger towns, most notably London; other areas continued to muddle through as best they could, either through inertia or financial hardship.

There is no doubt that the distressed areas came off worst in terms of health provision during the 1930s. A linked question is how far the unemployed suffered disproportionately. This can be looked at on three levels. First, it was claimed that unemployment led to psychological illness. This seems not to have been true, in most cases: provided people retained their family life and were not 'wrenched from their class and community', they escaped 'unscathed' (McKibbin, 1990, p. 258), although it should also be noted that means tests could have a disintegrating effect on family life, since the earnings of one's children were taken into account in assessing one's entitlement to benefit. Secondly, it was argued that unemployment caused physical infirmity. But although the numbers of people claiming sickness and disability benefits rose, this was partly because the economic recession combed out the less 'able' workers first; they then found it more difficult to find alternative employment due to the glut of workers already on the market. In addition, such benefits were something of a last resort for unemployed men and women who had found other avenues closed to them. Significantly, when labour was scarce again during the Second World War, this 'army of derelicts' who, it had been feared, would never work again, almost disappeared from view (Whiteside, 1987, p. 244). At most, existing ailments were aggravated by the stress and poverty associated with joblessness. Thirdly, it is difficult to sustain the argument that unemployment had an adverse effect on infant mortality rates. All too often the figures do not match the argument. For example, the rate fell in Northumberland in the early 1930s, in

Glamorgan in mid-decade, and in Durham immediately before the war, despite high unemployment (Winter, 1983, p. 247). The significant variations were less between the unemployed and those in work than between the social classes and between the regions. But this was nothing new, it has remained the case, and there is little hard evidence to suggest that things got worse in the 1930s. Nor was it only working-class women who died frequently in childbirth (Lewis, 1980, p. 220).

The nation's health improved quite drastically during and after the Second World War, largely because of prosperity and full employment; the construction of a more generous and universalist state-run welfare system (with the creation of the National Health Service, the institution of family allowances, and a much more comprehensive system of social insurance than had existed previously); and improved diet (due to rationing and free milk, orange juice, and cod-liver oil). How much of this could have been achieved in the 1930s? Probably very little. The National Governments believed they were already doing all they could to maximize employment; the creation of a welfare state was never on their agenda and, indeed, survey evidence suggests that there was no great working-class demand for such a structure, even though there was discontent with the existing system (Harris, 1983). There was more pressure for the introduction of family allowances, whereby all families would receive a flat-rate weekly payment for each child. This would solve the problem of family poverty, especially in larger families, in a way which would leave the existing wage structure intact. Such arguments aroused the hostility of trade unionists, who claimed that wages and not allowances should be the basis of the family economy. However, it was hard to see how a wage for a job could be related to size of family: if, for example, wages were set at a three-child standard, then they would be excessive for those with fewer than three children, and inadequate for those with more. The arguments in favour of family allowances were, in fact, very strong, and by the later 1930s a number of Conservatives were becoming convinced by them. But it was the war which brought them into being.

In the hospital sector, the trend in the 1930s was clearly

117

towards a larger input from the public sector, but the voluntary hospitals continued to thrive and there was little support for a system run totally by the local authorities even among advocates of a national health service. Here, too, it took the approach of war to change things: the setting up of the emergency hospital service seemed to many policy-makers to make a centrally-controlled national hospital service inevitable, but this was at least as much due to an acceptance of the fact that it would be very difficult to disaggregate the system after the war as to an ideological conversion to welfare politics: and issues like fees remained unresolved (Fox, 1986, p. 95). In addition, greater credibility was given to the relatively new science of nutrition by the time of the war; given the perceived need to restrict expenditure in the thirties, extensive dietary supplementation was not until then seen as a practical possibility. In other areas, like family planning, we should be even less censorious of 1930s policymakers: while some maternity and child welfare clinics gave birth control advice, they were strictly circumscribed, and the growth in the use of artificial contraceptives stemmed from sources other than the social services; the risky and often sexually unsatisfactory withdrawal method also remained widespread. Indeed, it was not until 1967 that local health authorities were allowed to give birth control advice on non-medical grounds and without reference to marital status (Lewis, 1980, p. 214).

Should we, then, be 'optimistic' or 'pessimistic' about health care in the 1930s? Clearly, the pessimists make some points which cannot be dismissed, especially regarding the depressed areas. There is no reason to doubt that life in many such areas was a catalogue of deprivation, distress, ill–health, and disadvantage. In addition, as seen in chapter 2, government was reluctant to take special measures to help those areas of the country in which a simple reliance on market forces would never be enough to produce economic revival. Even so, the pessimists' case does not really convince as a picture of the national scene. Most people did not live in depressed areas. Furthermore, most of the 1930s were not years of 'depression' in most of the country. It should also be stressed that even with the introduction of the welfare state in the 1940s there was still acute poverty among sections of the population, which hardly suggests that the problems of the 1930s were as easy to solve as the pessimists argue. In fact, the pessimists' case would be more convincing if one were not so frequently deafened by the sound of political axes being ground when one reads their writings. 'It is vitally important,' wrote Webster in 1982, 'that our thinking about the present phase of serious unemployment should not be clouded by a false perspective with respect to its most immediate ancestor and obvious analogue [the 1930s]' (p. 111). To some extent, then, it is history as political polemic; that does not make it bad history, but it does mean that we should treat its findings with some caution.

Broadly speaking, the 1930s saw an improvement in health and living standards for the bulk of the population, but there were pockets of deprivation. It is to impose a false perspective to argue that the latter were more significant than the former. At the same time, though, the government's concern for expediency and lack of idealism, and the increasingly self-congratulatory manner with which it defended its policies, created a legacy of resentment and mistrust, not least among those sections of the middle classes which were discussed above.

CONCLUSION

British society in the 1930s was generally becoming more prosperous and living standards for the majority were higher than ever before. This is not to deny that there were pockets of severe depression throughout the decade, or that working-class people, in particular, still suffered great economic uncertainty at times. Yet health improved; and there were also improvements in housing, although it should not be forgotten that the middle classes probably benefited most in this area, and that many people still lived in slums. The record since 1945 suggests that few periods have seen such encouragement for owner-occupiers at the same time as good-quality public housing was being constructed. And, of course, real incomes rose. One product of this was the considerable expansion of leisure.

119

Social policy was undynamic. However, here too there was some improvement in most areas. By 1940 there was a basis for the extension of provision by more hard-pressed and less pessimistic governments. It would be wrong to say that they intended it, but the National Governments had, indirectly, laid the foundations upon which a welfare state could be built.

British society was also, despite class divisions, essentially cohesive. It was this cohesion that allowed Britain to avoid the excesses of political extremism, and which was to help it to pull together so effectively once war came. But there was a catch. People were increasingly aware, through the mass communications revolution, of the living conditions of their fellow countrymen and women; and, as the nation became more prosperous, increasing numbers were asking if more could not be done to alleviate poverty, ill-health and unemployment. Even before the war, therefore, there existed a feeling, particularly among a minority of the middle class, that government was being over-cautious. It was that minority which was to help create and sustain much of the imagery of the 'Devil's Decade': that they were able to do so owed much to the outbreak of war in 1939 and its continuation for six years, for that 'proved' that the National Governments had been 'wrong' in foreign policy; hence, it could be argued, they had been 'wrong' in domestic policy as well. Be that as it may, it should not cloud our perceptions of what the 1930s were really like for the majority of the population.

5

Conclusion

What, to sum up, was the experience of Britain in the 1930s? Clearly, there was, and is, a lot to argue about, and it would be patently absurd to claim that so brief a survey as this can settle the arguments once and for all. Nevertheless, a number of points emerge which, when taken together, suggest that the decade had more good about it than bad, and that the writers who have been particularly pessimistic have been those with a personal prejudice, or those writing from a false perspective, or those for whom, one suspects, no real, existing society would ever be good enough.

The performance of the British economy during the decade was by no means unimpressive. The average annual growth rate of 2.2 per cent per annum between 1924 and 1937 compared favourably with earlier and later periods of prosperity. Real wages rose considerably until late in the decade, and then fell back only slightly. Trade revived substantially after the 1929–32 recession, and there was some movement from the staples towards 'new' industries. There were recessions, in 1929–32 and 1937–8, but the economy also experienced boom conditions all too rarely seen in the 1920s. This should not blind us, however, to the immense structural problems which the government faced, particularly the over-dominance of the ailing staple industries in certain parts of the country: this meant pockets of very high levels of long-term unemployment throughout the decade and was the reason why, even in boom conditions, almost one worker in ten was unemployed.

Economic policy was least successful in dealing with these structural problems. The faith in market forces, which worked well for most of the country, could never solve the problems of the depressed areas. A more active regional policy was needed than the Special Areas legislation introduced in 1934. Of course, the National Governments had little faith in it, and its main aim was to reassure National supporters in other parts of the country that *something* was being done. However, it would be wrong to judge them on the strength of regional policy alone. Cheap money, protectionism, a managed exchange rate, and the maintenance of business confidence through an ostentatiously-balanced budget all helped recovery after 1932, and provided a marked contrast with the failings of the 1929–31 Labour government. Since full cyclical employment was reached by early 1937, 'Keynesian' methods, even if they could have been implemented, would probably have fuelled inflation, worsened the trade balance by drawing in imports, and added to instability. The government's unspectacular economic policy served most of Britain well.

Domestic politics were not particularly inspiring either. One cannot easily imagine people being thrilled by the sight of Baldwin, being moved to euphoria by a speech from Attlee, or seeing Neville Chamberlain as a political role-model. Even the 'exciting' politicians were less so during the thirties: MacDonald was a sad shadow of his former self, Lloyd George was a rather pathetic figure whose histrionics and staged oratory simply did not move the viewers of newsreels, Churchill's behaviour seemed to defy analysis most of the time, and Mosley had moved so far from the accepted norms of political life that few people could take him seriously. But this did not matter much. The 'exciting' politicians of the decade were Hitler, Mussolini, Stalin; and while some contemporaries might have wished that one of them could have been in charge of Britain, this was not the view of the vast majority and it is not a view that the historian can endorse. Even the idea of the 'lost generation' was a myth, for those who had fought in the Great

War were not old enough to be at the helm of politics in the thirties: many older men had to be overcome before Eden, and still more Macmillan, could lead the Conservative Party. By the end of the decade both Labour and the Liberals had turned to men of that generation for their leadership, but that merely reflected the turmoil in which both parties spent much of the decade.

The basic facts of politics were that the Liberals were in sharp and irreversible decline, and became a mere irritant during the decade; that the extremist parties never had a hope of success; and that Labour, for all the changes it claimed to have wrought, was seen by substantial numbers throughout the thirties as the party of depression and governmental incompetence, a party proved 'unfit to govern' and whose performance gave too little reassurance even to many of its supporters that this was not, in fact, the case. By contrast, the cautious, pragmatic competence of the National Governments and the Conservative Party retained widespread support, even among sections of the unemployed, and, more generally, within the working class. It was not innovative, but it provided a degree of stability and prosperity which benefited all classes, though not all to the same degree.

For there remained gross inequality, and what would seem to us today searing poverty, affecting large numbers of people. Health care could have been more comprehensive; benefits could have been more generous, particularly for those, like the older long-term unemployed, for whom 'less eligibility' did not apply since they could find no work of any kind; there was ample room for improvement in the educational system; more help could have been given to the depressed areas. Yet it is important not to overstate the omissions of government policy, or to underplay what was achieved. Most people were in work, and for them real wages rose for most of the period; even when they fell slightly with price rises later in the decade, they were still comfortably above the levels of the 1920s, and the price inflation, ironically, was a concomitant of the government's policy of rearmament, which created more jobs. There were real advances in housing, particularly slum clearance on

123

a considerable scale, and even if owner-occupation was not extended as significantly as has sometimes been claimed to the working class, there were some gains here. Leisure was more varied and enjoyed by more people than ever before. Health did improve for the majority: even a pessimist like Mitchell, while denouncing conditions in the depressed areas, is forced to admit that there were 'undoubted improvements in conditions for the majority of working-class women and children' during the decade (1985, p. 119).

Social policy erred on the side of caution; but then again, there was a lot for government to be cautious about. It was terrified that another, worse, slump would follow any significant increase of government expenditure, and seen from the perspective of the 1930s that was a logical, if arguably wrongheaded, lesson to draw from the experience of Britain since 1918, and especially of the 1929–31 Labour government. Thus the priority had to be to restore economic health: only prosperity could pay for further reform (a view shared to a large extent by most Labourites for most of the decade). Later in the thirties, the priority had to be rearmament against the increasing threat from Germany. And, to turn Webster on his head, despite their attack on 'optimistic' views of the 1930s, few pessimists would press their case to the extent of claiming that the poor would have been lucky to have been alive under German occupation (cf. Webster, 1985, p. 205). Spending had to be prioritized, in the 1930s as at all other times: and, understandably, there were other priorities than social welfare expenditure. However there were some improvements, and by the end of the decade services were more comprehensive than ever before. It is only in contrast with what followed that they seem so inadequate.

All this has implications for a number of other things, too. First, the experience of Britain in the Second World War followed naturally from the experience of the 1930s. Society was not so deeply divided in the pre-war years that the country could not pull together once war had started in earnest. At the same time, it was not ripe for a social revolution, and so the effects of war were not all that dramatic. The many differences between the Britains of 1939 and 1951 were not as glaring as has sometimes been alleged, and again this can be traced back to the thirties. Secondly, the survival of parliamentary democracy during the war meant that there needed to be no great constitutional initiatives or changes after the war. Instead there was a continuity in politics, society, and economy which was seen as a boon at the time but which, in retrospect, might have prevented the fundamental changes that have so helped countries as diverse as West Germany, France, and Japan. However, the persistence of poverty, even under the post-war welfare state, suggests that the same phenomenon in inter-war Britain would not have been as easily curable.

Why, then, did the 1930s get such a bad press, particularly from middle-class intellectuals? Part of the answer has already been given, but one further aspect must be noted. The period was one governed by materialism rather than idealism; one where governments seemed to act according to pragmatisn rather than principle; and where people were becoming less sociable, more private, and hence, so it was felt, more selfish. During the 1940s, as the war brought people together and collectivism became the order of the day, there was a feeling that all this had changed. The idealistic middle-class party thrown up by the war, Common Wealth, seemed to encapsulate the transformation. One of its best-known posters consisted 'simply of the words "Is it expedient?" crossed out and replaced by "Is it right?"' (Orwell, 1970, p. 331). But the image of the 1940s as a decade of cosy consensus and brotherly and sisterly love is too simplistic, while the 1950s were to be notorious for their materialism. In that sense, then, the 1940s were the aberration; the fact that the myth of the 'Devil's Decade' took root in that decade should perhaps warn us against it still further.

The final point is a more general one. It is that people should be careful when writing recent or 'contemporary' history to ensure that they do not take too 'presentist' a view. In the 1950s and 1960s, it was taken as read by most historians that welfare politics and Keynesian economics 'worked'. Thus, to writers at that time, governments of the 1930s had been foolish, incompetent, or evil in holding fast to other economic ideologies.

125

Similarly, in the 1980s, when free-market economics were in vogue, there was a tendency to judge the 1930s from that standpoint. Webster, to repeat, presents his work on the thirties very much in terms of its being 'vitally important that our thinking about the present phase [to 1982] of serious unemployment should not be clouded by a false perspective with respect to its most immediate ancestor and obvious analogue' (Webster, 1982, p. 111). Both perspectives were somewhat false. The 1930s have suffered too much from people using them for their own purposes. They were, in fact, a period of economic, social, and political flux, and their end-product was a country which was, on the whole, better-off than it had been in 1929, ready to face the ultimate challenge of war in reasonably good shape. This is not to deny the existence or the seriousness of poverty, misery, and deprivation in some areas. But, that said, there are solid grounds for being 'optimistic' about the 1930s.

APPENDIX 1 GENERAL ELECTION RESULTS 1929–1945

	1924	1929	1931	1935	1945
Seats					
Conservative	412	260	470	387	197
National Labour	–	–	13	8	–
Liberal National	–	–	35	33	11
National	–	–	3	1	2
[Total National]	[n/a]	[n/a]	[554[a]]	[429]	[210]
Labour	151	287	46	154	393
Liberal	40	59	33	21	12
Communist	1	–	–	1	2
Other	11	9	15	10	25
Total	615	615	615	615	640
Votes					
%					
Conservative	46.8	38.1	55.0	47.8	36.2
National Labour	–	–	1.5	1.5	–
Liberal National	–	–	3.7	3.7	2.9
National	–	–	0.5	0.3	0.5
[Total National]	[n/a]	[n/a]	[67.2[a]]	[53.3]	[39.6]
Labour	33.3	37.1	29.3	38.0	48.0
Liberal	17.8	23.6	6.5	6.7	9.0
Communist	0.3	0.2	0.3	0.1	0.4
Other	1.8	1.0	3.2[b]	1.9	3.0
Total	100.0	100.0	100.0	100.0	100.0

[a] Liberals were part of the National Government at the time of the election but later moved into opposition.
[b] Includes the New Party (0.2), which won no seats. With this exception no Fascist candidates ran at the general election.

127

APPENDIX 2 UNEMPLOYMENT 1929–1940

(000)	January	July
1929	1,434	1,176
1930	1,534	2,072
1931	2,671	2,783
1932	2,794	2,889
1933	2,979	2,507
1934	2,457	2,185
1935	2,397	2,045
1936	2,229	1,717
1937	1,766	1,445
1938	1,927	1,875
1939	2,133	1,326
1940	1,602	898

Figures show the numbers of people registered at employment exchanges.
Source: *Ministry of Labour Gazette*, vols. 37–48 (1929–40)

References and Guide to
Further Reading

General books on the thirties are not thin on the ground. For
'traditional' views, see Muggeridge (1940), Branson and Heinemann
(1971), and Cockburn (1973). For the major 'revisionist' view, see
Stevenson and Cook (1977).

On the economy, a good general survey covering the period is
Aldcroft (1986). Pollard (1983) is full of useful information. On
policy, see Middleton (1985) and Tomlinson (1990); Peden (1985) is,
perhaps, more accessible. On the failed alternatives of these years,
see the excellent survey in Booth and Pack (1985).

On politics, the Conservatives are well-covered in Ramsden (1978).
For Labour, Pimlott (1977) is stimulating. The Liberals are less
well-served: see the relevant sections of Douglas (1970). On the
Communists, the standard work is now Branson (1985); for the other
extreme, see Thurlow (1987). For electoral politics, see Thorpe
(1991) and Stannage (1980).

On social history Stevenson (1984) provides a good survey. Perkin
(1989) is full of excellent insights on this period, while Routh (1980)
is highly informative. For social policy see Crowther (1988) and Fox
(1986). For housing, see Daunton (1984) and Merrett (1982). Leisure
is best covered by Jones (1986).

Acland, R. 1940: *Unser Kampf: Our Struggle*. Harmondsworth.
Aldcroft, D. H. 1986: *The British Economy, Volume 1: The Years of
    Turmoil 1920–1951*. Brighton.
Allen, G. C. 1970: *British Industries and Their Organization*. London,
    5th edn.

Attlee, C. R. 1949: *The Labour Party in Perspective*. London, 2nd edn.

Ball, S. 1988: *Baldwin and the Conservative Party: The Crisis of 1929–1931*. London.

Beales, H. L. and Lambert, R. S. 1934: *Memoirs of the Unemployed*. London.

Beard, M. 1989: *English Landed Society in the Twentieth Century*. London.

Bebbington, D. W. 1989: *Evangelism in Modern Britain: A History from the 1730s to the 1980s*. London.

Benson, J. 1989: *The Working Class in Britain 1850–1939*. London.

Booth, A. E. 1983: The 'Keynesian Revolution' in economic policymaking. *Economic History Review*, 36, 103–23.

Booth, A. E. 1989: *British Economic Policy, 1931–49: Was there a Keynesian Revolution?* London.

Booth, A. E. and Pack, M. 1985: *Employment, Capital and Economic Policy: Great Britain 1918–1939*. Oxford.

Bradley, I. 1982: *The English Middle Classes are Alive and Kicking*. London.

Branson, N. 1985: *History of the Communist Party of Great Britain, 1927–1941*. London.

Branson, N. and Heinemann, M. 1971: *Britain in the Nineteen Thirties*. London.

Burnett, J. 1978: *A Social History of Housing 1815–1970*. Newton Abbot.

Butler, D. E. and Butler, G. 1986: *British Political Facts 1900–1985*. London, 6th edn.

Calder, A. and Sheridan, D. 1984: *Speak For Yourself: A Mass-Observation Anthology, 1937–1949*. London.

Cannadine, D. 1980: *Lords and Landlords: The Aristocracy and the Towns, 1774–1967*. Leicester.

Capie, F. 1983: *Depression and Protectionism: Britain Between the Wars*. London.

Capie, F. and Collins, M. 1980: The extent of British economic recovery in the 1930s. *Economy and History*, 23, 40–60.

Carr-Saunders, A. M. and Wilson, P. A. 1933: *The Professions*. London.

Census 1931: England and Wales, *Occupation Tables*. London.

Cockburn, C. 1973: *The Devil's Decade*. London.

Cole, G. D. H. 1937: *The People's Front*. London.

Cook, C. 1976: *A Short History of the Liberal Party 1900–1976*. London.

Cook, C. and Ramsden, J. (eds) 1973: *By-Elections in British Politics*. London.

Cowling, M. 1975: *The Impact of Hitler: British Politics and British Policy, 1933–1940*. Cambridge.

Craig, F. W. S. (ed.) 1975: *British General Election Manifestoes 1900–1974*. Glasgow.

Cronin, J. E. 1984: *Labour and Society in Britain, 1918–1979*. London.

Crowther, A. 1988: *British Social Policy, 1914–1939*. London.

Curran, J. and Seaton, J. 1985: *Power Without Responsibility: The Press and Broadcasting in Britain*. 2nd edn, London.

Currie, R., Gilbert, A. and Horsley, L. 1977: *Churches and Churchgoers: Patterns of Church Growth in the British Isles since 1700*. Oxford.

Daunton, M. (ed.) 1984: Introduction in M. Daunton, (ed.), *Councillors and Tenants: Local Authority Housing in English Cities, 1919–1939*. Leicester, 1–38.

Dewar, H. 1976: *Communist Politics in Britain: The CPGB from its origins to the Second World War*. London.

Digby, A. and Bosanquet, N. 1988: Doctors and patients in an era of national health insurance and private practice, 1913–38. *Economic History Review*, 41, 74–94.

Douglas, R. 1970: *The History of the Liberal Party since 1895*. London.

Dresser, M. 1984: Housing policy in Bristol, 1919–39. In M. Daunton, (ed.), *Councillors and Tenants: Local Authority Housing in English Cities, 1919–1939*. Leicester, 156–216.

Drummond, I. M. 1981: *The Floating Pound and the Sterling Area 1931–1939*. London.

Durbin, E. F. M. 1990: *The Politics of Democratic Socialism*. London.

Finnigan, R. 1980: Housing policy in Leeds between the wars. In J. Melling, (ed.), *Housing, Social Policy and the State*. London, 113–38.

Fox, D. M. 1986: *Health Policies, Health Politics? The British and American Experience 1911–1965*. Princeton, NJ.

Freeden, M. 1986: *Liberalism Divided: A Study in British Political Thought 1914–1939*. Oxford.

Garside, W. R. 1985: The failure of the radical alternative: public works, deficit finance and British interwar unemployment. *Journal of European Economic History*, 14, 537–55.

Garside, W. R. and Hatton, T. J. 1985: Keynesian policy and British unemployment in the 1930s. *Economic History Review*, 38, 83–8.

Glynn, S. and Booth, A. E. 1985: Building counterfactual pyramids. *Economic Hisotry Review*, 38, 89–94.

Glynn, S. and Howells, P. G. A. 1980: Unemployment in the 1930s: the 'Keynesian Solution' reconsidered. *Australian Economic History Review*, 20, 28–45.

131

Gray, N. 1985: *The Worst of Times: An Oral History of the Great Depression in Britain*. London.

Harmer, H. J. P. 1988: The failure of the Communists: The National Unemployed Workers' Movement, 1921–1939: A disappointing success. In A. J. Thorpe, (ed.), *The Failure of Political Extremism in Interwar Britain*, Exeter, 29–47.

Harris, J. 1983: Did British workers want the welfare state? G. D. H. Cole's survey of 1942. In J. M. Winter, (ed.), *The Working Class in Modern British Politics: Essays in Honour of Henry Pelling*. Cambridge, 200–14.

HMSO, 1940: *Statistical Abstract of the United Kingdom 1924–1938*. London.

Humphries, J. 1987: Interwar house building, cheap money and building societies: the housing boom revisited. *Business History*, 29, 325–45.

Johnman, L. 1986: The largest manufacturing companies of 1935. *Business History*, 28, 226–45.

Jones, S. G. 1986: *Workers at Play: A Social and Economic History of Leisure 1918–1939*. London.

Klingender, F. D. 1934: *The Condition of Clerical Labour in Britain*. London.

Lewis, D. R. 1987: *Illusions of Grandeur: Mosley, Fascism and British Society 1931–1981*. Manchester.

Lewis, J. 1980: *The Politics of Motherhood: Child and Maternal Welfare in England, 1900–1939*. London.

Lewis, J. 1986: The prevention of diphtheria in Canada and Britain 1914–1945. *Journal of Social History*, 20, 163–76.

McKibbin, R. I. 1990: *The Ideologies of Class: Social Relations in Britain, 1880–1950*. Oxford.

McLeod, H. 1984: *Religion and the Working Class in Nineteenth-Century Britain*. London.

Marquand, D. 1977: *Ramsay MacDonald*. London.

Marwick, A. 1980: *Class: Image and Reality in Britain, France and the USA since 1930*. London.

Mason, T. 1989: Football. In T. Mason (ed.), *Sport in Britain: A Social History*. Cambridge, 146–86.

Mass-Observation, 1943: *The Pub and the People: A Worktown Study*. London.

Mayhew, M. 1988: The 1930s nutrition controversy. *Journal of Contemporary History*, 23, 445–64.

Merrett, S. 1982: *Owner-Occupation in Britain*. London.

Middlemas, K. 1979: *Politics in Industrial Society: The Experience of the British System since 1911*. London.

Middlemas, K. and Barnes, J. 1969: *Baldwin: A Biography*. London.

Middleton, R. 1982: The Treasury in the 1930s: political and administrative constraints to acceptance of the 'new' economics. *Oxford Economic Papers*, 34, 48–77.

Middleton, R. 1985: *Towards the Managed Economy: Keynes, the Treasury and the Fiscal Policy Debate of the 1930s*. London.

Mitchell, B. R. and Deane, P. 1962: *Abstract of British Historical Statistics*. Cambridge.

Mitchell, M. 1985: The effects of unemployment on the social condition of women and children in the 1930s. *History Workshop*, 19, 105–27.

Morgan, K. 1989: *Against Fascism and War: Ruptures and Continuities in British Communist Politics 1935–1941*. Manchester.

Mowat, C. L. 1955: *Britain between the Wars 1918–1940*. London.

Muggeridge, M. 1940: *The Thirties: 1930–1940 in Great Britain*. London.

Nicholas, K. 1986: *The Social Effects of Unemployment in Teesside, 1919–39*. Manchester.

Orwell, G. 1970: *The Collected Essays, Journalism and Letters of George Orwell, Volume 2: My Country Right or Left, 1940–1943*. Ed. S. Orwell and I. Angus. Harmondsworth.

Owen, A. D. K. 1931: *A Report on the Housing Problem in Sheffield*. Sheffield.

Peden, G. C. 1980: Keynes, the Treasury and Unemployment in the Later 1930s. *Oxford Economic Papers*, 32, 1–18.

Peden, G. C. 1983: Sir Richard Hopkins and the 'Keynesian Revolution' in employment policy, 1929–45. *Economic History Review*, 36, 281–96.

Peden, G.C. 1985: *British Social and Economic Policy*. Deddington, Oxon.

Pegg, M. 1979: British radio broadcasting and its audience 1918–1939. Ph.D. thesis, University of Oxford.

Pelling, H. 1958: *The British Communist Party: A Historical Profile*. London.

Perkin, H. 1989: *The Rise of Professional Society: England since 1880*. London.

Pilgrim Trust, 1938: *Men Without Work*. Cambridge.

Pimlott, B. 1977: *Labour and the Left in the 1930s*. Cambridge.

Pimlott, B. 1985: *Hugh Dalton*. London.

133

Pimlott, B. (ed.) 1986: *The Political Diary of Hugh Dalton 1918–1940, 1945–1960*. London.

Pinto-Duschinsky, M. 1981: *British Political Finance 1830–1980*. Washington, DC.

Pollard, S. 1983: *The Development of the British Economy 1914– 1980*. London.

Pronay, N. 1971: British newsreels in the 1930s: 1. Audience and producers. *History*, 56, 411–18.

Ramsden, J. 1978: *The Age of Balfour and Baldwin*. London.

Ramsden, J. 1987: 'A party for owners or a party for earners?' How far did the British Conservative party really change after 1945? *Transactions of the Royal Historical Society*, 37, 49–63.

Rhodes James, R. 1970: *Churchill: A Study in Failure 1900–1939*. London.

Richards, J. 1983: The cinema and cinema-going in Birmingham in the 1930s. In J. K. Walton and J. Walvin (eds), *Leisure in Britain 1780–1939*. Manchester.

Rollin, J. 1980: *Rothman's Football Yearbook 1980–1981*. London.

Ross, J. F. S. 1948: *Parliamentary Representation*. London, 2nd edn.

Routh, G. 1980: *Occupation and Pay in Great Britain 1906–79*. London, 2nd edn.

Rowntree, B. S. 1941: *Poverty and Progress: A Second Social Survey of York*. London.

Rowson, S. 1934: A statistical survey of the cinema industry in Great Britain in 1934. *Journal of the Royal Statistical Society*, 49, 67–119.

Royle, E. 1987: *Modern Britain: A Social History, 1750–1985*. London.

Rubinstein, W. D. 1981: *Men of Property: The Very Wealthy in Britain Since the Industrial Revolution*. London.

Rubinstein, W. D. 1986: *Wealth and Inequality in Britain*. London.

Saville, J. 1988: *The Labour Movement in Britain*. London.

Seymour-Ure, C. 1975: The press and the party system between the wars. In G. Peele and C. Cook (eds), *The Politics of Reappraisal*, London, 232–57.

Singer, H. W. 1940: *Unemployment and the Unemployed*. London.

Skidelsky, R. 1967: *Politicians and the Slump: The Labour Government of 1929–31*. London.

Skidelsky, R. 1975: *Oswald Mosley*. London.

Stannage, T. 1980: *Baldwin Thwarts the Opposition: The British General Electon of 1935*. London.

Stevenson, J. 1976: Myth and reality: Britain in the 1930s. In A.

Sked and C. Cook (eds.), *Crisis and Controversy: Essays in Honour of A. J. P. Taylor*. London, 90—109.

Stevenson, J. 1984: *British Society 1914—1945*. Harmondsworth.

Stevenson, J. and Cook, C. 1977: *The Slump: Society and Politics During the Depression*. London.

Swenarton, M. and Taylor, S. 1985: The scale and nature of the growth of owner-occupation in Britain between the wars. *Economic History Review*, 38, 373—92.

Symons, J. 1960: *The Thirties: A Dream Revolved*. London.

Taylor, A. J. P. 1965: *English History 1914—1945*. Oxford.

Thomas, J. H. 1937: *My Story*. London.

Thomas, M. 1983: Rearmament and economic recovery in the late 1930s. *Economic History Review*, 36, 552—79.

Thorpe, A. J. 1988: Introduction in A. J. Thorpe (ed.), *The Failure of Political Extremism in Interwar Britain*. Exeter, 1—10.

Thorpe, A. J. 1991: *The British General Election of 1931*. Oxford.

Thurlow, R. 1987: *Fascism in Britain: A History 1918—1985*. Oxford.

Tomlinson, J. 1978: Unemployment and government policy between the wars: a note. *Journal of Contemporary History*, 13, 64—78.

Tomlinson, J. 1990: *Public Policy and the Economy since 1900*. Oxford.

Waller, R. J. 1983: *The Dukeries Transformed: The Social and Political Development of a Twentieth Century Coalfield*. Oxford.

Ward Price, G. 1937: *I Know These Dictators*. London.

Webster, C. 1982: Healthy or hungry thirties? *History Workshop*, 13, 110—29.

Webster, C. 1985: Health, welfare and unemployment during the Depression. *Past and Present*, 109, 204—30.

Wertheimer, E. 1929: *Portrait of the Labour Party*. London.

Whiteside, N. 1987: Counting the cost: sickness and disability among working people in an era of industrial recession 1920—1939. *Economic History Review*, 40, 228—46.

Winter, J. M. 1979: Infant mortality, maternal mortality, and public health in Britain in the 1930s. *Journal of European Economic History*, 8, 439—62.

Winter, J. M. 1983: Unemployment, nutrition and infant mortality in Britain 1920—1950. In J. M. Winter (ed.), *The Working Class in Modern British History: Essays in Honour of Henry Pelling*. Cambridge, 232—56.

Index

British Fascisti 50, 51
British Medical Association 114
British Union of Fascists 50, 51−8,
    123; and Communists 42, 44,
    47−8; formation 27, 50, 51;
    Labour Party and 27, 32, 48;
    racism 54−5, 94; TUC ban 46;
    see also Mosley, Sir Oswald
budgetary policy 61, 71−2, 78−9,
    110, 122
building societies 98
Burnley, Lancs 98
businessmen 87, 88−9; see also
    confidence, business
Butlin, Billy 107

Cabinet, National Government
    12−13, 19, 36
Cable Street, Battle of 48, 55
Camping Club of Great Britain 107
capitalism 7, 8, 52; and
    development of socialism 23, 27,
    28, 32, 33, 62, 71
Catholic Church 24, 48, 103−4
Chamberlain, Neville: appeasement
    19−20; economic policies 71, 73,
    75; fall 2, 6, 59; and formation of
    National Government 10, 12;
    becomes premier 18−19; and
    regional policy 75; style of
    leadership 7−8, 18−19, 59, 122;
    and UAB 14
chemical industry 67
childbirth 111, 112, 113, 114, 117
churches: decline in attendance 94,
    102, 103−4, 107, 109, 110; and
    politics 15, 18, 24, 48
Churchill, Winston Spencer: and
    abdication crisis 18; and
    approaching war, 2, 20; as
    Chancellor of Exchequer 78;
    Coalition Government (1940) 6,
    40, 57; and free trade 9;
    historians' assessment 3; and
    India 9, 15; in wilderness 2, 9,

122
CI see Communist International
cinema 96, 103, 107−8, 109
Citrine, Walter 26
civil defence 20
Clacton-on-Sea, Essex 107
class, social 86−97, 117; see also
    individual classes
clerical workers 89−90
clubs, working-men's 103
coal industry 20, 65, 67, 93, 101
Coalition Governments: (1916−22)
    7, 33−4, 60, 63; (1940) 6, 40, 57
cohesion, social 94, 120, 124
Cole, G. D. H. 32−3
comics, children's 109
Comintern see Communist
    International
Common Wealth 125
communications, mass 107−9, 110,
    120; see also radio
Communism in Europe 56, 58
Communist International 42, 43,
    44−5
Communist Party of Great Britain
    41−9, 58, 123; 'class against
    class' line 41, 42−3, 44, 46; and
    Fascism 42, 44, 47−8; and
    Independent Labour Party 44;
    intellectuals 48−9; and Labour
    Party 28, 32, 41, 42−3, 44; and
    Liberals 44; Soviet control 42,
    43, 44−5; trade union policy 43,
    45−6; and unemployed 15, 42,
    46−7; united front policy 28, 32,
    41, 43, 44, 49; and War 44−5
community, sense of 101
confidence, business 63, 66, 71, 72,
    73, 78, 79, 122
Conservative Party: aristocrats and
    87; dissent within 2, 20−1, 123;
    economic policy, 1924−9, 62;
    and family allowances 117; and
    National Governments 7−22,
    123, (formation) 6, 9, 10−11,

137

139

140